The
Baptism,
Filling & Gifts
of the Holy Spirit

The Baptism, Filling & Gifts of the Holy Spirit

by

W. A. CRISWELL, Ph.D., D.D.
Pastor of the First Baptist Church
Dallas, Texas

Zondervan Publishing House • Grand Rapids, MI

MINISTRY RESOURCES LIBRARY is an imprint of Zondervan
Publishing House, 1415 Lake Drive, S.E.,
Grand Rapids, Michigan 49506

THE BAPTISM, FILLING AND GIFTS OF THE SPIRIT
© 1973 by The Zondervan Corporation
Grand Rapids, Michigan

Excerpted from
THE HOLY SPIRIT IN TODAY'S WORLD

ISBN 0-310-22751-8

Library of Congress Catalog Card Number: 66-29826
Printed in the United States of America

89 90 91 92 / EP / 22 21 20 19

Contents

Introduction

In the midst of a great deal of confusion arising out of the present discussion concerning the doctrine of the Holy Spirit and its meaning for contemporary man, Dr. W. A. Criswell speaks to the issue with the voice of Biblical authority and addresses himself to the sensitive areas of the Spirit's baptism, filling and gifts with the combined skill of an able exegete and lucid expositor.

The careful distinctions which the author draws between the baptism of the Spirit and His filling, between the gift of the Holy Spirit and His gifts to the church, and his extensive study of the much neglected theme of spiritual gifts, combine to make this volume one which merits the attention of Christians everywhere, especially those whose lives have been touched by the modern charismatic movement.

These chapters were originally prepared for delivery as a series of messages to the author's congregation, the First Baptist Church of Dallas, and were subsequently published in a larger book, *The Holy Spirit in Today's World*, through the sponsorship of Mr. James Cantrell. Because of the continuing need for Biblical material which will clarify the teachings of Scripture on this pivotal doctrine, Dr. Criswell has graciously given the publishers permission to excerpt the last sixteen chapters from his previously released larger book for publication in this paperback edition.

THE PUBLISHERS

Chapter 1

The Baptism of the Holy Spirit

Matthew 3

11 I indeed baptize you with water unto repentance: but he that cometh after me is mightier than I, whose shoes I am not worthy to bear: he shall baptize you with the Holy Ghost, and with fire.

The study of the New Testament presentation of the baptism of the Holy Spirit has brought astonishing, amazing discoveries to me. The truth is nothing as I would have expected. For one thing, the term as such is not found in Scripture. The term "the baptism of the Holy Spirit" is so much used and so greatly abused, but it is not in the Word of God. Only in reference to the prophecy of John the Baptist, concerning the ministry of Christ, is any mention made in the gospels or in the Acts to a baptism by the Holy Spirit. After reading Matthew 3:11 one would expect page after page in the four gospels to describe this marvelous experience. It is never referred to by name; it is never mentioned as such. After reading Acts 1:5 and Acts 11:16, one would expect to read in the Acts page after page of discussion concerning that baptism by the Holy Spirit. Again, it is never referred to by name; it is never mentioned as such. In fact, the word "baptize," with reference to the Spirit, is never used in recounting the story of Pentecost, of Samaria, of Caesarea, of Ephesus, or of anywhere else. This is amazing!

But what is more astonishing, we are never told, commanded, or urged to seek the baptism of the Holy Spirit. The idea is alien to the Scriptures. Some seek, pray, wait for such an experience. They are persuaded that God has reserved for a chosen few that unusual baptism. They expectantly, prayerfully, and sometimes agonizingly wait before the Lord for this heavenly gift. Some even build whole systems of theology upon it, presenting it in their teaching as a second work of grace. First, they say, we are regenerated (saved); then we are baptized by the Holy Spirit in a further, deepening consecration to God.

The Baptism by the Spirit
in the Gospels and the Epistles

When we seek the Scriptural truth concerning any such baptism of the Holy Spirit, we cannot find it in the gospels. There such an experience is not referred to save in John's prophecy (Matt. 3:11). Nor is the doctrine discussed in the Book of Acts. There, again, the subject is not referred to save in John's prophecy (Acts 1:5; 11:16). It is in the epistles that the doctrine is unfolded. This is not an accident. It is according to the studied purpose of God.

As we turn to the epistles, a multitude of questions crowd into our minds. What is the baptism of the Holy Spirit? When did it happen? When does it happen today? Who is the baptizer? Into what does He baptize? What are the results? Are there any signs accompanying such an experience? Let us begin our inquiry in the middle of the doctrine (some would say "controversy") and work out from there.

Who is the baptizer and with what does He baptize? In Matthew 3:11; Acts 1:5; 11:16, the three passages presenting the prophecy of John the Baptist, Jesus is unmistakably the baptizer and it could be that the Holy Spirit is the sphere into which He baptizes. But in the epistles, in 1 Corinthians 12:13, the Holy Spirit is the baptizer and the body of Christ is the sphere into which He baptizes. (1 Cor. 12:13: "For by one Spirit are we all baptized into one body.") Are there, then, two different baptisms, one by the Lord Jesus and one by the Holy Spirit? We might think so but for the fact that the same Greek phrase is used to describe both baptisms, en pneumati. Can we build two separate doctrines of the baptism of the Holy Spirit on the same Greek phrase, on the same Greek preposition? Many do so! These dualists interpret the Greek preposition en used in Acts 1:5 in a location sense, meaning a baptism into the sphere of the Holy Spirit. Then they interpret the same Greek preposition en used in 1 Corinthians 12:13 in an instrumental sense, meaning a baptism into the sphere of the body of Christ. The en employed in 1 Corinthians 12:13 is clearly and only instrumental. The baptizer is the Holy Spirit; it is He who does the baptizing.

But what of the prophecy of John the Baptist in Matthew 3:11 where Jesus is clearly presented as the baptizer? In what sense is He the baptizer? In answering this question, we shall find the answer as to why the Spirit baptism is not discussed in the gospels. The gospels present pre-ascension events (John 7:39). Before there can be a Spirit baptism, there must be an atonement made on earth for our sins and a justification declared in heaven for our souls. Before the Spirit can be poured out, Christ must be put to death, raised from the grave, and must ascend into heaven. Water baptism is that in picture; Spirit baptism is that in fact and reality. (Rom. 6:3-5; Col. 2:12, we are dead with Christ, buried with Christ, and raised with Christ.) The result of the death, burial, Resurrection, and Ascension of Christ will be the ascension gift, the promise of the Father, the outpouring of the Spirit. There is no outpouring of the Spirit, there is no ascension gift until Christ has died, been buried, been raised, and has ascended into heaven. After the gospels, after the Ascension, then the gift (John 16:7; Eph. 4:8). The coming of the Holy Spirit at Pentecost is the ascension gift of our Lord to His church.

In this sense, and only in this sense, is Christ the baptizer. He was the Giver of the original ascension gift. He sent the Paraclete to take His place. Through

and by Him the Spirit is poured out. But after the
Spirit's advent, the Spirit and not Christ is spoken of
as the baptizer. The agent and the instrument in the
baptism is the Holy Spirit (1 Cor. 12:13). In all instances and in all experiences, Christ is the ultimate
source or agent in the baptism by the Spirit, as Matthew 3:11 prophesies. Christ sent the Spirit. But as
Christ is the primary agent, so after Pentecost the
Holy Spirit is the immediate agent. The Spirit does
the actual baptizing, joining believers in Christ to His
body, the church.

The Time of the Baptism by the Spirit

We turn now to the question, when did and when
does the baptism occur? John the Baptist, in Matthew
3:11, announced the reality as something beyond himself and his ministry. Jesus in the flesh (John 14:16,
26) spoke of it as a future event. In Acts 1:5; Jesus,
raised from the dead but not ascended, referred to the
gift as immediately coming. Acts 11:16 speaks of the
baptism as having already taken place. The fulfillment
of the promise clearly occurred at Pentecost and continued thereafter, joining both Jews and Gentiles to
the body of Christ. This baptism of the Holy Spirit
is the new departure at Pentecost. It inaugurated the
present day of grace which was unknown in the days
of the Old Testament. The baptism of the Spirit places
believers in the body of Christ, the church. The church
is built upon the death, burial and Resurrection of
Christ and is an institution that had no breath of the
Spirit (John 20:22) until the ministry of our Lord
Jesus was complete. The church, including both Jews
and Gentiles, was unknown to the prophets. The institution was a secret hid in the heart of God (Eph.
3) and is distinctive of the present age.

The pouring out of the Spirit, the baptism of the
Spirit, occurred at a set date, by divine promise. It is
an ascension gift. The gift was not bestowed as a re-

10

ward for praying or for human merit. Christ was born at a set time, He was crucified at a set time, He was raised from the dead at a set time, He ascended into heaven at a set time, and He sent the Holy Spirit in accordance with the promise of the Father at a set time.

In Luke 24:49 the Lord told the disciples to tarry in the city of Jerusalem until the promise of the Father should be sent upon them. The Greek word translated "tarry" is *kathizo*, which means "to sit down," "to stay," "to remain." The disciples were not to attempt any work of witnessing (Acts 1:8) until the Holy Spirit came upon them. While they waited, they prayed, had fellowship, elected an apostle, spoke of Judas, and did other things; but all that was unconnected with the coming of the Holy Spirit. He came at a divinely scheduled time (Acts 2:1), at a divinely designated place (Joel 2:32. Had they been tarrying in another place except Jerusalem they would have missed the blessing), and in accordance with Old Testament types (Lev. 23:15-22).

The Spirit of Pentecost Is With Us Forever

The Holy Spirit, having come, is to be with the believer forever. John 14:16 promises, "And I will pray the Father, and he shall give you another Comforter, that he may abide with you for ever." There is to be no second Pentecost in the sense of an ascension gift inaugurating a new age. In the economy of God a second Pentecost would be as impossible as a second incarnation. The Holy Spirit is here without measure and with the followers of the Lord forever.

The blessed Spirit of Jesus is here with us now: "And I will pray the Father, and he shall give you another Comforter, that he may abide with you for ever; even the Spirit of truth; whom the world cannot receive, because it seeth him not, neither knoweth him: but ye know him; for he dwelleth with you, and shall be in you" (John 14:16, 17). Never again do we have to wait ten days or ten seconds. He indwells *now* every believer. The waiting now is on the part of the Holy Spirit to empower us, to fill us to the utmost. It is but for us to yield our souls, hearts, minds, bodies to the indwelling presence. Pentecost is with us all the time, every day and hour. We are to live every minute in the fullness of God. This accounts for the agony of our prayers: not that the Holy Spirit is reluctant to come (He is already here), but that we are reluctant to yield our members to Him. He possesses so little of us. Our sins blot Him out, as said the prophet Isaiah: "Behold, the LORD's hand is not shortened, that it cannot save; neither his ear heavy, that it cannot hear: But your iniquities have separated between you and your God, and your sins have hid his face from you, that he will not hear" (Isa. 59:1, 2). Sometimes we must wrestle through the night of despair as Jacob did at Peniel until broken and yielded we also cry, "I will not let thee go, except thou bless me" (Gen. 32:26). God grant to us this yieldedness of our lives that we might possess the fullness of the Spirit.

Chapter 2

The Results of the Baptism of the Holy Spirit

1 Corinthians 12

13 For by one Spirit are we all baptized into one body, whether we be Jews or Gentiles, whether we be bond or free; and have been all made to drink into one Spirit.

In this message we come to the heart and center of the doctrine of the Holy Spirit. The Scriptures are very plain in their teaching concerning the work of the presence of God in our lives. It is we who misunderstand, misappropriate, misuse, and misapply what the Bible has lucidly set before us. Following the Word of the Lord, we shall consider first what the baptism by the Holy Spirit is not; then we shall present what the baptism by the Holy Spirit is.

The Baptism of the Spirit Is Not Regeneration

Spirit baptism is not regeneration; it is not salvation. There is a vast difference between the two. The disciples were saved before Pentecost. The marvelous transformation that came into their lives at Pentecost was nothing short of miraculous but it was not salvation. They knew the Lord in His saving, forgiving grace before they gave themselves in prayer and to waiting for the promise of the Father. Regeneration is not baptism. In regeneration the believer accepting Christ is saved. Christ comes into his heart. He becomes a Christian through the committal of his life by faith to the Lord Jesus. Revelation 3:20 beautifully outlines what happens when a sinner opens the door of his heart and lets Jesus come in. "Behold, I stand at the door, and knock: if any man hear my voice, and open the door, I will come in to him, and will sup with him, and he with me" (Rev. 3:20). The appeal of the gospel song reflects the precious invitation of our Lord:

If you are tired of the load of your sin,
Let Jesus come into your heart;
If you desire a new life to begin,
Let Jesus come into your heart.

Just now your doubtings give o'er
Just now reject Him no more;
Just now throw open the door,
Let Jesus come into your heart.

That is salvation, letting Jesus come into your heart. But by Spirit baptism, the believer is placed "in Christ." Galatians 3:27 reads: "For as many of you as have been baptized into Christ have put on Christ." The Greek word translated "have put on Christ" is *enduno*, which literally means in this verse "to clothe one's self with." We are in Christ as we are in our clothes. We are clothed in Christ. Spirit baptism places us there. This difference between regeneration by the Spirit and baptism by the Spirit is seen in John 14:20, "At that day ye shall know that I am in my Father, and ye in me, and I in you." "I in you" is regeneration. "Ye in me" is the baptizing work of the Holy Spirit.

In regeneration the soul is quickened from death to life. Paul writes in Ephesians 2:1, "And you hath he quickened, who were dead in trespasses and sins." In salvation the Spirit imparts life. In Spirit baptism the believer is taken out of the old creation of death in Adam and placed eternally in the new creation of life in Christ. This is marvelously illustrated in the picture of baptism in Romans 6:3-5.

Know ye not, that so many of us as were baptized into Jesus Christ were baptized into his death? Therefore we are buried with him by baptism into death: that like as Christ was raised up from the

14

dead by the glory of the Father, even so we also should walk in newness of life. For if we have been planted together in the likeness of his death, we shall be also in the likeness of his resurrection.

This new creation into which the believer is introduced is also seen in 2 Corinthians 5:17:

Therefore if any man be in Christ, he is a new creature: old things are passed away; behold, all things are become new.

In regeneration the believer is made a child of God (John 1:12; Gal. 3:26). He is made a joint-heir with Christ (Rom. 8:16, 17). In Spirit baptism the child of God is made an organic part of the body of Christ.

For by one Spirit are we all baptized into one body, whether we be Jews or Gentiles, whether we be bond or free; and have been all made to drink into one Spirit (1 Cor. 12:13).

The Baptism by the Spirit
Is Not the Anointing

Spirit baptism is not the anointing. It is most common for Bible teachers to say that Jesus was baptized with the Holy Spirit following His water baptism in the Jordan River. One great preacher writes, "Jesus never entered His public ministry until He was baptized with the Holy Spirit." No, Jesus was anointed by the Holy Spirit as He stood before John in the Jordan. He was divinely filled without measure (John 3:34). Spirit baptism is a result of Christ's finished work of redemption. It is an ascension gift. The purpose of the Spirit baptism (1 Cor. 12:13) is to join us to Christ as Christ is joined to the Father. Christ needed no such baptism. He needed not to be joined to the Father. He was already one with the Father. What happened, then, at Jesus' baptism when "the Holy Spirit descended in a bodily shape like a dove upon him . . ."? (Luke 3:22; cf. Matt. 3:16). The answer is plain. Jesus was anointed for His holy, Messianic office upon which He was now entering. The

15

coming of the Holy Spirit upon Him was His consecration to the priesthood as He prepared to offer the sacrifice which will wash our sins away. The Levitical law required all priests to be consecrated when they began to be about thirty years of age (Num. 4:3; Luke 3:23). The Levitical consecration for the priesthood was two fold: there was first a washing in water; then there was the anointing with oil (Exod. 29:4, 7; Lev. 8:6, 12). In His water baptism Jesus identified Himself with sinners. He was baptized — washed with water. He was then anointed with the Holy Spirit. He was consecrated — set apart — for the holy office to which He had committed His life.

Spirit baptism is not the sealing whereby Christ stamps us as His own for eternity. It is not the indwelling whereby Christ grants us His continuing presence. It is not the filling. There is one baptism; there are many fillings. There is no command, ever, to be baptized by the Holy Spirit. There is distinct injunction for every believer to be filled with the Spirit. Because in two instances (at Pentecost and at Caesarea) the baptism by the Holy Spirit and the filling of the Holy Spirit occurred at the same time, Bible teachers have made the two the same. This is a tragic error. The baptism is not the filling.

By the Baptism We Are Joined to the Body of Christ

What, then, is baptism by the Spirit? The all-important answer to this question is found in these Scriptures: 1 Corinthians 12:13; Romans 6:3-5; Galatians 3:27; Ephesians 4:5; Colossians 2:12; 1 Peter 3:21. According to 1 Corinthians 12:13 the baptizing work of the Holy Spirit has to do with the Church, the body of Christ. We repeat, the baptizing has to do with the Church. By the Spirit baptizing we are joined to the body of Christ. We are baptized into the Church. Never is it said in Scripture that anyone is baptized into the Holy Spirit. We are never baptized, placed, immersed in the Spirit. The Spirit is the baptizer. He is the instrument, the agent, who places the believer into the body of Christ. The creation of this one body, the Church, was a mystery hid through the ages in the heart of God (Eph. 3:3, 5, 6, 9, 10). The prophets of the Old Testament never saw it. It was hid from their eyes. That Gentiles were to be saved was no mystery (secret kept in the heart of God). Moses (Deut. 32:21), Isaiah (42:6, 7; 65:1), Hosea (2:23), Joel (2:28-32), and others had told of Israel's blindness and the subsequent mercy to the Gentiles. But that there was to be a Church, a body into which both Jews and Gentiles were to be baptized, was a mystery (secret) hidden in the counsels of the Almighty. The creation of that one body is the result of the baptizing work of the Holy Spirit.

In the creation of one unity with many believers, three figures are used. One figure is that of a bride (Rev. 21:9, 10). An angel said to John the Seer, "Come hither, I will show thee the bride, the Lamb's wife." And when John was carried away in the Spirit to a great and high mountain, and saw that fabulous bride, what he saw was the Holy City, "descending out of heaven from God" (Rev. 21:10). All the saved in Christ Jesus, the bride with her friends and companions and guests, live in the beautiful city. Together they comprise the New Jerusalem. Another figure representing this unity in Christ, the result of the baptizing work of the Holy Spirit, is that of a building. Christ is the foundation (1 Cor. 3:11), and we are the living stones built upon the foundation to make up the holy Temple of God. (1 Peter 2:4-7). A third figure presenting this baptizing work of the Holy Spirit is that of a body. Christ is the head (Eph. 1:22), and we are different members of that one body (Eph. 5:23; 1 Cor. 6:18; 12:13-27). At the moment of our salvation the baptizing work of the Holy Spirit joins us as a living member to the body of Christ.

This creative, uniting work of the blessed Spirit is wrought by a "separation from" and a "joining to." Romans 5 and 6 present a contrast between the sinner "in Adam" and the saint "in Christ." The sinner in the old Adam's nature is under the condemnation of death. The saint in the new nature is not only saved, justified, delivered from death into everlasting life, but is, "in Christ," joined to the living body of our Lord. Thus we read in 1 Peter 3:20, 21 that baptism is a type of deliverance out of death into life. The waters of the flood separated the eight from the perishing world. They, the saved, were in the ark, "in Christ." Our being "in Christ," the result of the baptizing work of the Holy Spirit, is all significant, eternally important. Noticeable in the list of the things that unite the body into one organic structure (Eph. 4:3-6) is the "one baptism." There is one baptism, the operation of God's Spirit, which places the believer in Christ, in His mystical body, of which the one water baptism is a symbol. We are saved, regenerated, born again; then we are baptized, added to the Church, the body of Christ.

The Baptism by the Spirit
Is Universal Among All Believers

The baptism by the Holy Spirit is experienced among all believers. Galatians 3:26, 27 says: "For ye are all the children of God by faith in Christ Jesus. For as many of you as have been baptized into Christ have put on Christ." 1 Corinthians 12:13 reads: "For by one Spirit are we all baptized into one body, whether we be Jews or Gentiles, whether we be bond or free; and have been all made to drink into one Spirit." The Scriptures expressly state that all born-again believers have been baptized into the one body of Christ. Paul did not exhort the Christian believers to be baptized in order to be more spiritual. He simply states that all had been baptized (Greek ebaptisthemen, aorist tense). Notice to whom Paul is addressing these

18

words. He is writing to a troubled, disordered, carnal church. They were divided over personalities, comparing one preacher, as Apollos, to another, as Paul. They were divided over doctrine, some holding to the truth, others to rank heresy. They were divided over practices, some even desecrating the Lord's table. They were divided over discipline, some even condoning gross incest. They were divided over legal matters, some carrying others into court. Yet, the Apostle states that they had all been baptized by the Holy Spirit.

This explains why there is an amazing absence of exhortation in the Scriptures that we get baptized by the Holy Spirit. The baptism is already a universal gift of God to all believers. We need not seek it, pray for it, try to achieve it, or receive it. We already have it. It is but now for us to take possession of our possession, to act upon the promises. We are but to yield to the heavenly power, to seek the fullness, to obey God's Word, to do God's will, to exercise prevailing prayer. The baptism of the Spirit is come. We have it and we have Him.

There was a time when the Holy Spirit as a heavenly fire was a mysterious force, flashing like lightning in the skies; we knew not why nor whither. He came now upon a Moses and again upon an Elijah. Sometimes the celestial force would strike out in Israel's camp in the destroying flame of God's anger. Sometimes the fire would fall upon a Mount Carmel in awesome majesty, consuming the altar along with the sacrifice. Sometimes the fire would appear in the burning bush at Horeb, sometimes as the blessed Shekinah glory in the temple, the strange, mysterious symbol of Jehovah's presence. But since Christ's Ascension, the Holy Spirit is poured out upon us all (Joel 2:28). He is with us and within us forever. For power, for conquest, for glory, we have received the baptism by the Holy Spirit. According to our faith and our yieldedness, we are able to do great and mighty things for Him.

Chapter 3

The Baptism and the Filling

Acts 2

¹ And when the day of Pentecost was fully come, they were all with one accord in one place.

² And suddenly there came a sound from heaven as of a rushing mighty wind, and it filled all the house where they were sitting.

³ And there appeared unto them cloven tongues like as of fire, and it sat upon each of them.

⁴ And they were all filled with the Holy Ghost, and began to speak with other tongues, as the Spirit gave them utterance.

Studying the Scriptures closely, intently, has changed not only my understanding of the work of the Holy Spirit in our hearts, but also the very language and nomenclature of that work. Much of the description I have used heretofore concerning the baptism of the Holy Spirit has been incorrect; many of the doctrinal statements I have followed are not Scriptural. When we let the Bible say what it says, an amazing overhauling of our systematic theology comes to pass.

Incorrect Interpretations of Scripture

Having committed myself to the presentation of the work of the Holy Spirit as the doctrine is revealed in the Scriptures, I can now easily see the twisting of interpretation on the part of preachers and theologians toward preconceived, self-chosen ends. The results of this willful misconstruction of the Word of God are seen in the vast confusion and spiritual helplessness all around us. As an example of plain, unadulterated, false exegesis of the inspired Word presented in defense of a false doctrine, let me quote from a page in a book written by a world-famed English scholar-

20

preacher. He writes: "In 1 Corinthians 12:13 Paul says, 'For by one Spirit are we all baptized into one body. . . .' Here the King James version uses the preposition 'by' — 'by one Spirit are we all baptized.' However, the preposition used in the original Greek is the preposition *en* — 'in one Spirit are we all baptized.' Unfortunately, the accident that the King James translators used the phrase 'by one Spirit' has given rise to some strange doctrines which suggest that the Holy Spirit Himself is the agent who does the baptizing. Had the authors of these strange doctrines paused long enough to consult the original Greek text, they would have found no basis or suggestion of any such doctrine. In fact, the whole teaching of the entire New Testament in this connection agrees in this fact, clearly and emphatically stated: Jesus Christ Himself alone — and no other — is the One who baptizes in the Holy Spirit." "The theologian who writes the above words supposes we have not looked at the original Greek text. That is the point. We have. And it is the looking at that Greek text that has changed our ideas of the baptism and the filling of the Holy Spirit."

The Greek preposition translated by the King James version in 1 Corinthians 12:13 with the English word "by" ("by one Spirit") is the Greek word *en*. Thayer's *Greek Lexicon of the New Testament* lists forty-four different uses of the preposition *en* besides page after page of other shades of meaning. The word *en* can be translated "in," "upon," "among," "before," "by," "during," "with," according to its context. Is there an instrumental use of the preposition *en* whereby it is translated "by"? Yes, indeed, and this most exclusively and emphatically. Look at Matthew 12:27, 28; 21:23, 24; 23:16-22; Acts 4:12; Romans 5:9, 10; 12:21; Revelation 13:10. In each instance (and these are but a few chosen from a legion of passages) the word *en* can mean only the instrumental "by." For one passage typical of them all, take the last one cited, Revelation 13:10: "He that killeth *en* [the Greek word] the sword must be killed en [the Greek word] the sword." The preposition is solely instrumental. It cannot mean "in." The verdict of the scholastic world would no less certainly translate the Greek word en in 1 Corinthians 12:13 with the English instrumental word "by" ("by one Spirit are we all baptized . . ."). The baptizing is done by the Holy Spirit. He is the agent and He baptizes us into the body of Christ.

The tremendous emphasis of the Scriptures is not upon the baptizing work of the Holy Spirit but upon the filling. Notice again the text in Acts 2:4, "And they were all filled with the Holy Spirit. . . ." The passage does not read here or anywhere else, "And they were all baptized with the Holy Spirit. . . ." There is no such language in the Bible. But what is said here is repeated again and again, "And they were all filled with the Holy Spirit." From the prophecy in Matthew 3:11 and Acts 1:5, one would suppose that exhortation after exhortation, plea after plea, would have been made that we be baptized with the Holy Spirit, that we constantly seek this baptism. The subject is never mentioned. It is never referred to, not by even a syllable of one word in any sentence. But the injunction that we be filled with the Holy Spirit is plainly stated (Eph. 5:18). And the record that the disciples were repeatedly filled with the Holy Spirit is the recurring theme in the story of the early church.

The Difference Between the Baptism and the Filling

In order that we might plainly and accurately see the difference between the baptism by the Holy Spirit and the filling of the Holy Spirit, let us list five major differences between the two. First, there is no command, ever, for anyone to be baptized with the Holy Spirit. But every believer is under commandment to be filled with the Spirit. The verb in Ephesians 5:18 (Greek, plerousthe) is in the imperative mood and present tense. It refers in Greek to continuous, repeated action. We are constantly being filled by the Holy Spirit.

Second, the baptizing work of the Holy Spirit is a once-for-all operation. It happens at the time of conversion. We are baptized once when we are saved; thereafter, we are never baptized again. The Greek verb used in 1 Corinthians 12:13 (abaptisthemen) is in the aorist tense, the Greek way of expressing a once-for-all experience. On the other hand, the filling of the Holy Spirit is again and again. The present tense is used in Ephesians 5:18, denoting continuous, repeated action. There is one baptism; there are many fillings. The once-for-all baptism of the Holy Spirit places us in the body of Christ (1 Cor. 12:13). If this could be repeated, it would mean that a person could be placed in the body of Christ; then removed from that body; then reinstated by a second baptism. Such a fanciful idea is foreign to Scripture. It is not the plan of life that we cut off a hand, or a foot, or an arm, or a leg, and that we replace the member. The member is given to us one time to stay. It is thus with us who are added as members to the body of Christ. It is not the purpose or even the contemplation of Scripture that we be cut off, then added back again. There is one Lord, one faith, one baptism (Eph. 4:5). Having been baptized one time, the baptism is never repeated. We are born into the family of God. We cannot unborn ourselves. That new birth is never repeated. But the great work of the Spirit is filling us, and the mighty personal experience of being filled may happen again and again. We never reach some elevated plain where God has nothing more for us. Through the power of the blessed Spirit I may have reached a glorious height yesterday, but there are even more celestial heights for me to reach today.

A third difference between the baptism and the filling lies in its positional, experiential aspect. The baptism of the Holy Spirit is positional, like writing our names in the Book of Life up in heaven. It is something God does for us in establishing our relationship with Christ and with the fellow members of Christ's body. The filling of the Holy Spirit, however, is experiential. The experience has to do with divine empowerment. It radically affects Christian life and service. The filling of the Holy Spirit is truly Pentecostal as Acts 2:4 graphically avows.

A fourth observation concerning the baptism and the filling is self-evident when we see the results of the two. The baptism places us in the body of Christ and, as such, places us in a position to receive power, but it does not in itself bestow or guarantee that power. The Corinthians had been baptized (1 Cor. 12:13) but they were grossly carnal (1 Cor. 3:1, 2; 5:1; 6:1). The Galatians had been baptized by the Spirit, they had put on Christ (Gal. 3:27), but they were in the very act of apostatizing (Gal. 1:6; 4:9). There is nothing in the baptism, as such, that gives power. But the filling is just the opposite. The filling is power itself. It is victory, conquest, march, missions, everything the Christian needs to do valiant service for the Master. Compare Peter the Coward in Matthew 26:69-75 with Peter the Bold in Acts 2:4, 14, 23, 37; 4:8. (If I were a teenager following the story of the crowing of the rooster, I would say, "Compare Peter the Chicken in Matthew 26 with Peter the Lion in Acts 2"!) The tremendous, miraculous difference seen in Peter is explained by the filling recorded in Acts 2:4 at Pentecost. We have a like record of victorious power in the story of the deacons in Acts 6: 3-8, 15; again in the story of Stephen in Acts 6:5; 7:55; again in the summary of the life of Barnabas in the beautiful verse of Acts 11:24; again in the life of Paul in Acts 9:17-22; 13:9. These fillings brought unusual power in witnessing and in missionary conquest.

A fifth and a last difference between the baptism of the Spirit and the filling of the Spirit can be most

24

effectively demonstrated in the Pentecostal second chapter of the Book of Acts. What happened at Pentecost? What did the disciples experience on that fiftieth day? In answer, can we trust the Word of God for what came to pass? Or shall we place man's word in God's mouth? Let God say what He says. It is when we do this that we see with amazing clarity that the word "baptize" is never used at Pentecost (nor in any other like situation). What is the word used? It is the word "filled" (Acts 2:4 as in Acts 4: 8, 31; 7:55; 8:17; 9:17; 10:44; 11:15; 19:6). The fulfillment of Matthew 3:11 and Acts 1:5 was found in the ascension gift of Christ upon His return to heaven wherein He poured out the Holy Spirit in keeping with the promise of the Father. Thereafter the work of the Holy Spirit is one of creating the new and divine institution, the Church which is the body of Christ. The Third Person of the Trinity regenerates the new members in Spirit conversion and adds them to the body in Spirit baptism. He has been doing that since Pentecost added three thousand converts to the household of faith. This is the baptism of the Holy Spirit fulfilling Matthew 3:11 and Acts 1:5.

But something else happened at Pentecost. What was it? It was the glorious experience recorded in the Pentecostal chapter, verse four: "And they were all filled with the Holy Spirit." The baptism added to the body, but the filling wrought wonders in the church. As a result of the filling, Acts 2:4 states that the disciples witnessed in foreign languages; Acts 2:11 describes their praising the wonderful works of God; Acts 2:14 presents their intrepid boldness in preaching; Acts 2:42 outlines their steadfastness in doctrine; Acts 2:44, 45 delineates their unselfishness of heart, and Acts 2:46 speaks of their glorious gladness of ecstatic worship. Oh, the glory of the fullness of the Spirit! O God, do it again and again and yet again! Do it now! Fill us with the power and presence of the blessed Spirit!

Chapter 4

The Command to Be Filled With the Spirit

Ephesians 5

18 And be not drunk with wine, wherein is excess; but be filled with the Spirit.

The Greek words used in this pointed command are *plerousthe en pneumati,* "to be filled with the Spirit." Aside from the fact that through inspired writers God employed the Greek language to create His New Testament, the words in the original language are most interesting and meaningful in themselves. Let us look at the mandate closely.

There Are Several Different Kinds of "Fillings"

There are several Greek words that can mean "fill." One is *kortazo,* which is always used with reference to hunger. Look at Matthew 5:6; 14:20; Luke 16:21; John 6:26; James 2:16; Revelation 19:21. Another word is *pletho* (from *pimplemi*), which is a factual word to describe the filling of anything with something else. In Luke 4:28 the city of Nazareth was "filled" with anger. In Luke 5:7 both ships were "filled" with the large catch of fish. In John 19:29 (Matt. 27: 48) the sponge was "filled" with vinegar. In Acts 19: 29 the whole city of Ephesus was "filled" with confusion. The word is used to record the factual filling by the Holy Spirit in such passages as Luke 1:15; 41; Acts 2:4; 4:8, 31; 9:17; 13:9.

A kindred word to the above *pletho* is the verb *pleroo.* It is the verb used in this command in our text, Ephesians 5:18. Thayer's Greek *Lexicon of the New Testament* has a long, involved discussion of the usages of this Greek word. Of prophecies and promises, it means "to bring to pass," "to accomplish"

26

(Matt. 1:22; 2:15; Acts 1:16). Of a ministry, it means "to complete it," "to fulfill it" (Acts 12:25; 14:26; Col. 4:17; Rev. 3:2). Of God, it means "to pervade," "to fill with His presence, power and activity." In Ephesians 1:23; 4:10 the exalted Christ, the head of the Church, "fills" the universe. In Ephesians 3:19 the Lord takes possession of the heart, soul and life, "filling" the whole personality. It is thus the verb is used in Ephesians 5:18. To be filled with the Holy Spirit means for us to be so controlled and motivated with the presence and power of the Spirit until our whole being is one perpetual psalm of praise and service to God (Eph. 5:19-32).

God Commands That We Be
Filled With the Spirit

Notice that the word *plerousthe* is in the imperative mood. It is a mandate. There is never a command that we be baptized by the Spirit, or that we be sealed or indwelt by the Spirit. These are positional; they refer to something God does for us, as writing our names in the Book of Life. The command that we be filled with the Spirit relates not to our position before God but to our daily service and walk. For, you see, a believer can be a carnal, worldly, unfruitful Christian. The New Testament looks upon a man as a trichotomy. He is made up of three parts. There is the *somatikos* man, the body man (from *soma*, "body") (1 Tim. 4:8). There is the *psukikos* man, the sensuous, volitional man (from *psuche*, the self as the seat of the affections and will) (1 Cor 2:14). There is the *pneumatikos* man, the spiritual man (from *pneuma*, "breath," "spirit") (1 Cor. 2:15). But the Christian believer, this *pneumatikos* man, can be also a *sarkikos* man, a fleshly, carnal man (from *sarx*, "flesh") (1 Cor. 3:4). The carnal man lives by the power and dictates of the flesh. The truly spiritual man lives by the power and dictates of the Spirit of God (Gal. 5:16, 17).

27

The Filling a Repeated Experience

Notice that the verb *plerousthe* is in the present tense. "Tense" to us in the English language means "time." We cannot say anything in English without placing it in some "tense," in some time, as past, present, future. But what we call "tense" in Greek verbs is not "tense" at all. Greek verbs express kinds of action, as a point (aorist), continuous as going on (present), having been completed and remaining completed (perfect), etc. This verb *plerousthe*, therefore, being in what is called the present tense, refers to enduring, continuous action. The translation literally would be, "Be ye being continuously filled with the Holy Spirit." The experience is repeated again and again. A Christian living a normal life of moment by moment yieldedness to God experiences a moment by moment fullness of the Spirit. Some men experience a spectacular, miraculous, unique fullness that stands out over all other fillings like a mountain peak in a lofty range, like the lone grandeur of a Kilimanjaro in Africa or a Fujiyama in Japan. Such men of marvelous witness and testimony are John Wesley, Charles G. Finney, Dwight L. Moody, and R. A. Torrey. They had one great filling of the Spirit that stood out above all others. (Some of them, as R. A. Torrey, wrongly call it "the baptism of the Holy Spirit.") But most of us experience the filling of the Spirit in repeated succession like a mountain chain of many equal peaks. Each day's work brings its measure of endowment and inspiration.

Notice that the verb *plerousthe* is plural in number. The command is addressed not only to the pastor, the preacher, the deacon, the Sunday school teacher, but to every Christian and to every church member. The Ephesian letter from which this text is taken is a circular letter. When Paul wrote it, he most likely left the salutation blank whereby the name of the church could be later inserted. In some ancient manuscripts the word "Ephesus" is omitted. In other ancient manuscripts the name "Laodicea" is written in, most certainly in keeping with the Laodicean letter referred to in Colossians 4:16. All of this gives emphasis to the fact that the injunction that we be filled with the Spirit is addressed to all churches, all readers, all Christians everywhere through all times and generations.

The Man Under the Influence of the Spirit

Notice lastly, that the verb *plerousthe* is in the passive voice. The subject is acted upon (as in English grammar, the passive voice is illustrated in the sentence, "He is carried," "He is swept away"). It is we who are acted upon by the Holy Spirit. In the complete text, "And be not drunk with wine, wherein is excess; but be filled with the Spirit," Paul is using an illustration of a man who is acted upon, dominated, controlled by something other than himself. The comparison is between the man under the influence of alcohol and the man under the influence of the Holy Spirit. Paul describes the man under the domination of alcohol as "asotia," translated "excess" but a word which really refers to "a course of abandonment" (cf. Titus 1:6; 1 Peter 1:4). When the man is drunk with wine and is given over to the influence of liquor, he is a changed person. Sometimes a most neatly groomed and dressed individual becomes disheveled, untidy, and downright dirty. Sometimes a shy, reticent man now talks loud and laughs uproariously. Sometimes a fellow who would never sing in his life now sings at the top of his voice. Sometimes a poor creature so inhibited that he is afraid of his own shadow now becomes as bold as a lion with courage to attempt anything. I heard about two inebriates, one of whom leaped out the window to fly around the block. In the hospital, when the other one came to see him, the much bandaged and broken up patient said to his friend, "Why did you let me do it?" His friend replied, "I thought you could!" Under the domination of the Holy Spirit, we also are changed persons. We are doing what we never thought of doing. We are saying what we never thought of saying. We are attempting what we never thought of attempting. In God we are different, changed people.

At Pentecost the ascended Saviour poured out the Holy Spirit upon the world without measure (John 3: 34). He is here in all His heavenly presence and miracle-working power. Having come, the Spirit jealously desires the whole of us. James, the Lord's brother and the pastor of the Church at Jerusalem, wrote a tremendously strong statement in James 4:5, "The spirit that dwelleth in us lusteth to envy." The Greek verb translated "lusteth" is *epipotheo* which means "to desire earnestly," "to long for." In 1611, when the King James version of the Scriptures was made, the word "lusteth" was an exact translation of *epipotheo*. But "lust" to us today has come to have another and unspiritual meaning. James meant that the Holy Spirit so desires to possess us that He envied other loves and interests that command our affection. Think of it! The Holy Spirit of God envying anything that we love more than Him! The verse is enough to make us weep for contrition in our very souls.

For the Spirit to have us, we must yield ourselves to Him. We must be emptied of self to be filled with all of His fullness. Our hands cannot be filled with other things if they are to know the fullness of God. Our hearts cannot be filled with worldly affection and ambition if we are to possess the Spirit without measure. Our souls must be emptied of self when we bring them to the fountains of heaven for the blessing. It seems that Paul's motto was "not I but Christ" (Gal. 2:20). Oh, that we could surrender ourselves to a like commitment! As we grow in grace, maybe at first it was all of self and none of Thee. Then, it was some of self and some of Thee. Then it was less of self and more of Thee. But now, God grant it, it is none of self and all of Thee. "Filled with the Spirit."

Chapter 5

The Second Blessing

Acts 8

⁴ Therefore they that were scattered abroad went everywhere preaching the word.

⁵ Then Philip went down to the city of Samaria, and preached Christ unto them.

⁶ And the people with one accord gave heed unto those things which Philip spake, hearing and seeing the miracles which he did.

⁷ For unclean spirits, crying with loud voice, came out of many that were possessed with them: and many taken with palsies, and that were lame, were healed.

⁸ And there was great joy in that city.

¹⁴ Now when the apostles which were at Jerusalem heard that Samaria had received the word of God, they sent unto them Peter and John:

¹⁵ Who, when they were come down, prayed for them, that they might receive the Holy Ghost:

¹⁶ (For as yet he was fallen upon none of them: only they were baptized in the name of the Lord Jesus.)

¹⁷ Then laid they their hands on them, and they received the Holy Ghost.

The success of Philip the Evangelist (one of the seven men of God ordained in the Jerusalem church) in Samaria was nothing short of phenomenal. The whole city where he was preaching turned to Jesus and there was joy and gladness on every hand. It was real revival. Preparation for the wonderful harvest of souls had been made by the Saviour in His visit to Sychar (John 4:1-42). John 4:25 presents the Samaritan expectation of a coming Messiah, an expectation as deep and as vivid as that entertained by the Jewish nation itself. When Acts 8:12 carefully notes that "they were baptized, both men and women," I could hope that included in this great company of believers was the woman Jesus talked to by the well. With the Lord's blessing upon them all, no wonder "there was great rejoicing in that city."

Note the divine change in the preaching of the Gospel found in the Samaritan revival. In Matthew 10:5 Samaria, as well as the Gentiles was expressly forbidden to the ministering apostles. The Lord said, "Go not into the way of the Gentiles, and into any city of the Samaritans enter ye not." That exclusion has now passed away. After the death, burial, Resurrection, and Ascension of Christ, the Gospel is to be progressively delivered to the whole earth. Beyond Jerusalem it is to be preached in Judaea; beyond Judaea in Samaria; beyond Samaria "unto the uttermost part of the earth." This emphatically reminds us that we must interpret any passage of Scripture in its context, in the day and way and purpose for which it was written. To note this dispensational change in preaching the Gospel to the Samaritans is most vital here as we shall see later on.

When news of this marvelous Samaritan revival came to the ears of the apostles at Jerusalem, they sent two of their number, Peter and John, to look up the results personally. This is doubly interesting in view of the fact that John, with his brother James, wanted Jesus to call down fire from heaven to consume a Samaritan village that refused to receive the Saviour (Luke 9:52-56). But it is a new day now. When Peter and John arrived and had witnessed for themselves the grace of God upon the new converts, they prayed for them that they might receive the Holy Spirit (for as yet He had fallen upon none of them). "Then laid they their hands on them, and they received the Holy Ghost" (Acts 8:15-17).

32

The Differing Interpretations
of the Samaritan Revival

The interpretations of this coming of the Holy Spirit upon the Samaritans are literally legion in number. The passage is used to bolster a thousand differing doctrines. Some appeal to the text to demonstrate the superiority of the bishop to the pastor (the Jerusalem apostles over the local Samaritan leadership). Some see in the story an illustration and confirmation of apostolic succession in ordination to the ministry. Recently, I attended a Cathedral Whitsunday service (commemorating the descent of the Holy Spirit at Pentecost) and listened to the bishop's sermon. He used this chapter in Acts to "prove" that only through the laying on of hands by the apostles and their successors could there be any valid ordination. Some appeal to this passage for the Biblical basis of the rites of confirmation. Actually and historically, this is the doctrinal starting point for what afterward developed into the ritual known as "confirmation." In modern usage it becomes the confirming of the promises made by the parents for the infant when the child was christened. Some see in the text "the second blessing" — saved then sanctified. The first work of grace, they say, is seen in the conversion of the Samaritans. The second work of grace, they avow, is seen in the coming of the Holy Spirit upon them. Some use the text as a defense for speaking in unknown tongues. To these interpretors, speaking in tongues is a sign of the descent of the Spirit upon the individual life. Tongues are not mentioned here, but these doctrinarians are most positive that there could be no other sign that the new converts had received the Spirit other than their speaking in unknown tongues. And thus on and on the discussions continue. It all reminds me of a Hindu fable called "The Blind Men and the Elephant" that the poet John Godfrey Saxe wrote down in verse. The story goes like this, a story which the author applied to theological differences:

THE BLIND MEN AND THE ELEPHANT

It was six men of Indostan
To learning much inclined,
Who went to see the Elephant,
(Though all of them were blind)
That each by observation
Might satisfy his mind.

The *First* approached the Elephant,
And happening to fall
Against his broad and sturdy side,
At once began to bawl:
"God bless me! but the Elephant
Is very like a wall!"

The *Second*, feeling of the tusk,
Cried, "Ho! what have we here
So very round and smooth and sharp?
To me 'tis mighty clear
This wonder of an Elephant
Is very like a spear!"

The *Third* approached the animal,
And happening to take
The squirming trunk within his hands,
Thus boldly up and spake:
"I see," quoth he, "the Elephant
Is very like a snake!"

The *Fourth* reached out an eager hand,
And felt about the knee.
"What most this wondrous beast is like
Is mighty plain," quoth he;
"'Tis clear enough the Elephant
Is very like a tree!"

The *Fifth* who chanced to touch the ear,
Said: "E'en the blindest man
Can tell what this resembles most;
Deny the fact who can,
This marvel of an Elephant
Is very like a fan!"

The *Sixth* no sooner had begun
About the beast to grope,
Than, seizing on the swinging tail
That fell within his scope,
"I see," quoth he, "the Elephant
Is very like a rope!"

And so these men of Indostan
Disputed loud and long,
Each in his own opinion
Exceeding stiff and strong
Though each was partly in the right,
And all were in the wrong!

The Moral:
So oft in theologic wars,
The disputants, I ween,
Rail on in utter ignorance
Of what each other mean,
And *prate about an Elephant
Not one of them has seen!*

God's Choice of Peter and the Apostles

Although I run the risk of being the *Seventh* Blind
Man to examine the elephant, I have a very definite
persuasion concerning the meaning of this story in Acts
8. Looking at the narrative in its context, as a part
of a greater whole, I can see that it follows in its order
the sovereign choice of God for us and our lives. It
is the Father's will that we have the greatest of all
gifts, the ascension gift of Christ, which is the Holy
Spirit in our hearts. This purpose of God for us is
promised again and again (Matt. 3:11; Luke 11:9-13;
24:49; John 20:22; Acts 1:4, 5). But God chose a
sovereign procedure by which the gift is to be com-
municated to the world and to us. The Lord made
the solemn promise to Peter and to the apostles that
the keys of the kingdom to open the door of salvation
to the hosts of the earth would be placed in their
hands. The promise was made to all the apostles in

35

Matthew 18:18, and emphatically and especially to Simon Peter in Matthew 16:18, 19: "And I say also unto thee, That thou art Peter, and upon this rock I will build my church; and the gates of hell shall not prevail against it. And I will give unto thee the keys of the kingdom of heaven: and whatsoever thou shalt bind on earth shall be bound in heaven: and whatsoever thou shalt loose on earth shall be loosed in heaven." The holy promise was not made to Philip or to any of the seven. It was most distinctly made to Peter and to the apostles.

In each instance, as the gospel message proceeded outward in accordance with the commission recorded in Acts 1:8 (Jerusalem, Judaea, Samaria, uttermost part of the earth), God sovereignly used Peter and the apostles as instruments through whom the Holy Spirit was introduced to the believers. In Acts 2:14 Peter, in his Pentecostal sermon, addresses his audience with these words, "Ye men of Judaea, and all ye that dwell at Jerusalem . . ." The keys of the kingdom were used herein to announce the opening of the door of salvation and the coming of the Spirit of grace to the Jewish nation. In Acts 10:28, 44-48 a like marvelous gift was extended through Peter to the Gentiles. So vivid was Peter's vision concerning the Gentiles and so mightily did God open the door to them in the descent of the Holy Spirit, that Peter not only ably defended his visit to the pagans in Acts 11, but he refers to God's sovereign choice of him as the heavenly instrument for this blessing in his address at the Jerusalem Conference in Acts 15:7: "And when there had been much disputing, Peter rose up, and said unto them, Men and brethren, ye know how that a good while ago God made choice among us, that the Gentiles by my mouth should hear the word of the gospel, and believe." It is Peter and the apostles whom God used throughout this expansion of the gospel ministry, according to His holy promise in Matthew 16:19 and Matthew 18:18.

Following the order stated in Acts 1:8, and true to His promises in Matthew 16:19; 18:18, God bestowed the Holy Spirit upon the Samaritans through Peter and his fellow Apostle, John. God did not give the Holy Spirit through Philip. God did not do it through any of the seven. According to the outline in Acts 1:8, God did not open the door through any other leader or prophet or evangelist. God had said He would do it through Peter and the apostles; and here in Samaria, to the Samaritans; as at Jerusalem, to the Jews; as at Caesarea, to the Gentiles; God is keeping His promise. The keys of the kingdom, the opening of the door of salvation, and the gift of the Spirit of grace to the nations is through the Apostle Peter. God chose him (Acts 15:7). The record here in Acts 8 confirms that choice. We must always remember that the Book of Acts is a transitional Book. The history recounts the transition from Judaism to Christianity, from Jew to Gentile, from law to grace, from Jerusalem to Antioch, from Judaea to all the world. Acts 8 is a part of that transitional experience. After the transition is made and the door of salvation is opened and the spirit of grace has come, Peter is not mentioned again in the record of Acts after chapter twelve, save for his defense of what he had done in welcoming the Gentiles in Acts 15. But in the transition period, of which Acts 8 is a part, Peter and not Philip was the sovereign choice of God through whom the gift of the Spirit was made.

The Repeated Blessings of the Holy Spirit

As we reread the story, therefore, in Acts 8, of the revival under Philip, and the coming of the Holy Spirit under Peter and John, are we to conclude that there are two distinct experiences of grace for the believer, a first and a second blessing? Is there an experience of salvation and also an experience of sanctification? Is there a gift for believers when they accept Christ, then a special gift for a special few which second blessing is received later in Christian experience? Having been saved, are we also to seek a second gift of the Spirit?

Many use the verse in Acts 19:2 to confirm the reality of such a second experience. "He said unto them, Have ye received the Holy Ghost since ye believed? And they said unto him, We have not so much as heard whether there be any Holy Ghost." Recently, I received a tract with the title printed in bold letters on the front page: "Have Ye Received the Holy Ghost Since Ye Believed? Have You?" The title is most arresting and is designed to startle almost any Christian believer. Unfortunately for the author of the tract, however, the New Testament was not written in the Elizabethan English of 1611 but in the Koine Greek of the first century. The Greek verb Paul used in his question to the twelve Ephesian disciples of John is *pisteusantes*, an aorist participle meaning "having believed." Paul asked, "Back there when you believed, did you receive the Holy Spirit?" There is no hint or approximation of the meaning "*since* ye believed" in the text at all. Paul wanted to know if they were truly converted or not, and to him the sign of a genuine conversation is the reception of the Holy Spirit in the believer's heart.

We are to have the Holy Spirit, "having believed," according to Paul's query in this passage in Acts 19:2. His presence is the sign of our salvation. Receiving the Holy Spirit is associated with repentance, faith and salvation. This is distinctly stated in Acts 2:38, in 1 Corinthians 12:13, and here in Acts 19:2. The gift of the Holy Spirit is not related as such to our progressive, experimental sanctification. As in the passage of our text in Acts 8:4-8, 14-17, the Spirit was not given Philip's converts because of their spiritual maturity. Some of them had just been saved; they were babes in Christ a few hours old. Nor was the gift of the

Spirit bestowed upon them because of their knowledge of the Word, nor because they had agonized in prayer, nor because of their complete spiritual dedication and separation from the world. The experience was a gift from heaven, sovereignly bestowed.

The gift of the Holy Spirit is for us when we repent, believe, trust and are saved. Jesus bestows the Holy Spirit without measure (John 3:34). The Holy Spirit is a person. He is here, all of Him. His possession of us may be partial but our possession of Him is total. He is with His saved always, fully, completely, eternally. But we deny Him ourselves. We refuse Him access to all the compartments of our hearts. We keep Him out of so many areas of our lives. But when we yield our members to Christ, we receive a second blessing. And when we further yield our members, we receive a third blessing. And when we further yield, we receive a fourth blessing.

Do I believe in a second blessing? Yes, indeed! Does the Scripture teach a second blessing? Yes, indeed! And the Holy Bible also teaches a third blessing, and a fourth, and a hundredth, and a thousandth. As we keep on yielding and surrendering, the Holy Spirit keeps on blessing, on and on and on, again and again and again. Oh, for the constant refilling of the Spirit!

Chapter 6

The Gift and the Gifts

Notice the singular use of the word "gift" in Acts 2:38:

> Then Peter said unto them, Repent, and be baptized every one of you in the name of Jesus Christ for the remission of sins, and ye shall receive the gift of the Holy Ghost.

Notice the singular use of the word "gift" in Acts 10:45:

> And they of the circumcision which believed were astonished, as many as came with Peter, because that on the Gentiles also was poured out the gift of the Holy Ghost.

Notice the singular use of the word "gift" in Acts 11:17:

> Forasmuch then as God gave them the like gift as he did unto us, who believed on the Lord Jesus Christ; what was I, that I could withstand God?

Now, notice the plural use of the word "gifts" in 1 Corinthians 12:1:

> Now concerning spiritual gifts, brethren, I would not have you ignorant.

Notice the plural use of the word "gifts" in 1 Corinthians 12:4:

> Now there are diversities of gifts, but the same Spirit.

The Scriptures differentiate clearly between "the gift of the Holy Spirit" and "the gifts of the Holy Spirit."

The "gift" (singular) is the indwelling of the Holy Spirit whereby He comes to take up residence in the heart of the believer the moment that believer accepts Christ as Saviour. The "gift" is for salvation to the lost. The Paraclete comes at conversion (Acts 2:38). He comes in the new birth (John 3:5). He comes once for all (1 Cor. 12:13), that He may abide with us forever (John 14:16). The "gifts" (plural) are imparted to the saved by the Holy Spirit for service in the Church. The child of God is to stir up, to kindle his gift and not to neglect it (2 Tim. 1:6).

The Gift of the Spirit in This Age of Grace

We discuss first the gift of the Holy Spirit. The outpouring of the Spirit of God is the supreme characteristic of this marvelous, glorious age in which we live. This is the age of grace, the age of the Holy Spirit, an age of the most blessed opportunities God has ever laid before man. Jesus said of John the Baptist that he was the greatest man born of woman; then the Master added, "nothwithstanding he that is least in the kingdom of heaven is greater than he" (Matt. 11:11). John did not live to see this incomparable age in which we live. He died before the cross, before the Resurrection, before the Ascension, before the outpouring at Pentecost. He was denied the privilege of becoming a part of the Church, the body of Christ. But we have that holy privilege, and as great as was the noble Baptist, we are greater because of our celestial position in Christ. As a disciple of Christ, the least, humblest Christian can possess the fullness of the Holy Spirit without measure. In the Old Testament the Holy Spirit came mightily upon men at different times and in different places. In the New Testament He dwells mightily within men through the centuries. In the Old Dispensation He descended upon men for certain purposes. In this New Age of Grace, since Pentecost He saturates men,

41

indwells men, to the praise and glory of God. In the Book of Judges, "the Spirit of the Lord came upon" Othniel (3:10), Gideon (6:34), Samson (13:25; 14: 19; 15:14). But in the Book of Acts, all may possess the divine Presence without hindrance or fear. Men, women, young, old, servants, masters, boys, girls, all may possess the riches of the gift to the utmost (Acts 2:16-18).

The resurrected Lord Jesus said to His disciples in John 20:22, "Receive ye the Holy Ghost." The Greek verb is *labete*, second aorist imperative active of *lambano*, and the first meaning of the verb is "take," "seize." Jesus breathed on His disciples and said, "Take ye the Holy Spirit." Sometimes we tremble before the proffered gift. We shrink from taking the priceless possession offered by the hand that was pierced to purchase it. And sometimes, just as we by faith reach forth our hands to grasp it, we shrink back saying, "I am not worthy; it is to much for me." Recently, I looked upon the dazzling riches of the Russian Czars displayed in the armory in the Moscow Kremlin. I thought of a story of the great Emperor Alexander. In the presence of his body guard he turned one time and presented to one of his humblest, most menial servants a magnificent golden cup. The poor vassal drew back and said, "Your Majesty, it is too much for me to take." The Czar hesitated, then thrusting the chalice into the hand of his servant replied, "But it is not too much for me to give!" We also shrink from taking the precious gift of the Holy Presence, saying, "I am not worthy; it is too much for me." But Jesus, with His nail-pierced hands stained with the blood that purchased it for us, presses the gift into our hands saying, "Take it! Take it! It is not too much for me to give." Let us look up into the face of our Saviour and say, "O blessed Lord Jesus, unworthy as I am, I take it." The gift is ours forever for the receiving. O wonderful, wonderful Lord! Bless His name, O my soul!

We need but to consent to receive the Holy Spirit *now*. There need to be no struggling, no waiting, no agonizing. Just abandon yourself to Him. Let Him fill you, possess you, like breathing deep of celestial air. "And he breathed on them and said, Take ye the Holy Spirit." Did the disciples wait for the gift ten days after the Ascension of our Lord? Yes, because the outpouring of the Spirit is an ascension gift, the beginning of this new age, this new dispensation. But now He is come. Pentecost has happened. The Holy Spirit has already been poured out upon us. We need not wait ten seconds for Him. The soul that consents *now* will be filled *now*. A humble preacher attending a gathering of his denomination spoke to the gifted preacher who had just delivered the message of the hour and said, "I am so glad I consented." The great preacher asked, "To what did you consent?" The humble man replied: "I had agonized for fifteen years, wanting to be filled with the Holy Spirit. Then I heard you say, 'Just consent to be filled and you will be filled.' I abandoned myself to God. I consented and I was filled. Oh, I am so glad I consented." Each time at a convocation of the brethren this humble brother would seek out the great preacher and say, "I am so glad I consented." In telling the story, the great preacher said, "And when I meet my brother in heaven I expect to have him stop me on one of those golden streets and say, 'Oh, I am so glad I consented!'" The gift of the Holy Spirit has been bestowed. We have but to take it. I do not know the author of this poem, but whoever he was, he knew the truth of the Holy Spirit of God.

O Heavenly Father, Thou hast told
Of a gift more precious than silver or gold;
A gift that is free to every one
Through Jesus Christ, Thy only Son.
Thank Thee, Lord, for the gift to me.
Thou hast said, I must believe;
It is only "take" and I shall receive.

43

If Thou didst say it, it must be true,
And there is nothing else for me to do.
I praise Thee, Lord, for the gift to me.
So I come to take, because my need
Is very great and real indeed.
On the strength of Thy word, I rise and say,
"O thank Thee, Lord, for the promise today,
The Holy Spirit given to me."

The Meaning of the Gifts of the Spirit

We turn now to the "gifts" (plural) of the Holy Spirit. The words used to describe these gifts are most pertinent. In 1 Corinthians 12:1 the Greek is *ta pneumatika*, literally "the spirituals." Paul literally wrote, "Now concerning the spirituals, brethren, I would not have you ignorant." In 1 Corinthians 12:7 he defines "the spirituals" as "the manifestation of the Spirit to every man to profit withal." These gifts are impartations of the Holy Spirit and are not to be confused with natural talents. An unbeliever, an atheist, an infidel, the vilest sinner, may have many congenital endowments. They are not *ta pneumatika*, spiritual gifts. The latter are bestowed by the Paraclete upon the believer for service in the Church, the body of Christ.

Paul uses yet another word to describe these gifts of the Holy Spirit to the members of the churches. He calls them, in 1 Corinthians 12:4, 9, 28, 30, 31, *ta charismata*, literally "grace gifts." The singular form of the word is *to charisma*. The word, *charisma*, is obviously related to *charis*, "grace," "the free, unmerited favor of God." (The beautiful name, Karen, given some of our children, is the accusative form of that Greek word, *charis*, "grace.") In the New Testament the use of the word *charisma* is quite extensive, ranging from the gift of salvation (Romans 6:23) to the gift of God's providential care (2 Cor. 1:11). But usually the word is used of special gifts given to man by God and, with the exception of 1 Peter 4:10, is used

44

only in the New Testament by the Apostle Paul. Here again we must remember that the word does not refer to a natural talent. It refers to a grace gift, an undeserved favor from God to man. It refers to something bestowed that is neither purchased nor merited; it is given freely of God. Some men are naturally gifted, of high intelligence, possessing natural endowments. These are not *ta charismata*. The *charismata* are supernatural endowments.

In one instance, in Romans 1:11, we find both words, *pneumatika* and *charismata* used together. The King James version reads, "For I long to see you, that I may impart unto you some spiritual gift. . . ." Paul literally wrote, "For I long to see you, that I may impart unto you some 'grace gift of spiritual manifestation.' "

These charismatic gifts are bestowed by Christ upon His Ascension into heaven. They could be also called "ascension gifts." Paul writes in Ephesians 4:7, 8, 11, 12:

> But unto every one of us is given grace according to the measure of the gift of Christ. Wherefore he saith, When he ascended up on high, he led captivity captive, and gave gifts unto men. And he gave some, apostles; and some, prophets; and some, evangelists; and some, pastors and teachers; For the perfecting of the saints, for the work of the ministry, for the edifying of the body of Christ.

All *pneumatika*, all spiritual gifts are based upon the victory of Christ upon the cross. Jesus entered into contest with Satan, death and the grave, and was victorious over all. Therefore, He has the right to distribute the spoils, to dispense these marvelous presents. The poet so beautifully writes:

> These gifts of grace He gave to His redeemed,
> When He ascended to His throne on high.
> They are His work, His wisdom, and His might;
> The power of His truth and love; indwelling light
> That fills the Church of Christ, the perfect man.

45

The Gifts of the Spirit
Are Sovereignly Bestowed

The gifts of the Holy Spirit are sovereignly bestowed. Look closely at 1 Corinthians 12:7, "But the manifestation of the Spirit is given to every man. . . ." And look even more closely at 1 Corinthians 12:11, "But all these worketh that one and the selfsame Spirit, *dividing to every man severally as he will.*" The Greek verb is *bouletai,* as "He chooses," as "He wills." The choice of our gifts is made by the Holy Spirit. We can ask, we can pray, we can covet a gift (1 Cor. 14: 39) but the decision lies beyond us. The power of choice is not ours and does not function at our behest. That is why envy, boasting, superiority, contumely are so out of place in the churches of our Lord. Paul wrote of this needed humility so effectively in 1 Corinthians 4:7: "For who maketh thee to differ from another? and what hast thou that thou didst not receive? now if thou didst receive it, why dost thou glory, as if thou hadst not received it?" All that we have in the kingdom and patience of Jesus is given us by His gracious love. There is no room for personal boasting. The gifts are not even bestowed as rewards. They are not indications of spiritual excellence or superiority. They are meted out to us "as the Spirit will." They are not bestowed because we have sought them. They are not to be vaingloriously sought by men. Although we can ask in prayer, we do not receive them because we prayed for them or coveted them. They are sovereignly bestowed. So many tarry, pray, weep, beg, agonize for some spiritual gift. They are not so obtained. When Paul wrote in 1 Corinthians 12:31, "But covet earnestly the best gifts," he was writing to a church that was emphasizing the least and the lowest gifts to the loss and deprecation of the most useful and profitable gifts. Paul is admonishing the church that it magnify the greatest gifts among its members (such as prophecy), not the least and last gifts (such as speaking in tongues). The gifts among the members were sovereignly bestowed by the Holy Spirit, but the church, according to Paul, was to magnify and greatly to use the most profitable gifts bestowed.

No one person has all the gifts but each member has at least one or more. Paul further writes in 1 Corinthians 12:27-30:

> Now ye are the body of Christ, and members in particular. And God hath set some in the church, first apostles, secondarily prophets, thirdly teachers, after that miracles, then gifts of healing, helps, governments, diversities of tongues. Are all apostles? are all prophets? are all teachers? are all workers of miracles? Have all the gifts of healing? do all speak with tongues? do all interpret?

Each gift is needed and is not to be neglected. Every member is essential to the body. No great church became that way on a one-man ministry. All, each, every one, great, small, rich, poor, old, young, have essential parts. Each one will possess an inner witness of the Spirit concerning the special gift that is his, and that inner witness will be corroborated, recognized, by the assembly of the saints. It was a surprised George W. Truett who was told by the Whitewright Baptist Church that he was to be ordained to the gospel ministry. The young man replied, "But I have sought to be a lawyer." The church answered, "But God has called you to be a preacher." And they thereupon proceeded to ordain him! Others will know of your gift.

God has a purpose in bestowing these charismatic gifts. They are for service. Let us read again 1 Corinthians 12:7, "But the manifestation of the Spirit is given to every man to profit withal." They are "given to every man to profit withal." Let us read also Acts 1:8, "But ye shall receive power, after that the Holy Ghost is come upon you: and ye shall be witnesses unto me both in Jerusalem, and in all Judaea, and in Samaria, and unto the uttermost part of the earth." The Lord did not say alone, "Ye shall be witnesses. . . ." But He did say, "Ye shall receive power . . . and [then] ye shall be witnesses. . . ." That statement still stands unaltered. Neither that commission nor the provisions to carry it out have been withdrawn. These spiritual gifts are the endowments of God to make us able to do His work in the earth. Paul was not stressing secondary things when he wrote 1 Corinthians 12:1, "Now concerning spiritual gifts, brethren, I would not have you ignorant." Nor was he advising a small and meaningless thing when he urged Timothy to stir up the gift that was in him (2 Tim. 1:6). These gifts are God's enablement for His disciples to evangelize the world.

Chapter 7

The Wonderful "Charismata"

1 Corinthians 12

1 Now concerning spiritual gifts, brethren, I would not have you ignorant.

Paul writes that he would not have us ignorant of the gifts of the Spirit. But I do not know any one thing in the realm of the ecclesiastical world about which we are more ignorant. We need to know, desperately so, the truth God would reveal to us about these *pneumatika*, these *charismata*, these "charismatic spirituals."

Four places in the letters of Paul are these gifts of the Spirit listed; namely, in Romans 12:6-8; 1 Corinthians 12:8-10, 28-30; and Ephesians 4:11. In Romans 12:6-8 they are named as follows:

1. Prophecy
2. Ministering
3. Teaching
4. Exhortation
5. Giving
6. Ruling
7. Showing mercy

In 1 Corinthians 12:8-10 they are named as follows:

1. Words of wisdom
2. Words of knowledge
3. Faith
4. Healing
5. Working miracles
6. Prophecy
7. Discerning spirits
8. Tongues
9. Interpretation of tongues

In 1 Corinthians 12:28-30 they are named as follows:

1. Apostles
2. Prophets
3. Teachers
4. Miracles
5. Healings
6. Helps
7. Governments
8. Tongues
9. Interpretation

49

In Ephesians 4:11 they are named as follows:

1. Apostles   4. Pastors
2. Prophets   5. Teachers
3. Evangelists

The total of all the gifts named comes to thirty. About eleven of these listed are duplicates, leaving something like nineteen different gifts mentioned by the Apostle Paul.

Typical Groupings of the Gifts of the Spirit

It is interesting to read learned discussions of these *charismata* and to note how each scholar will group them in his own way. Here, for example, is one grouping:

   I. Gifts for the Ministering of the Gospel
       Those listed in 1 Corinthians 12:8-10

  II. Gifts for the Work of the Church
       Those listed in 1 Corinthians 12:28-30

 III. Gifts for the Ministries of the Church
       Those listed in Romans 12:6-8

 IV. Gifts for the Building Up of the Church
       Those listed in Ephesians 4:11

Another scholar has followed a unique outline in 1 Corinthians 13 and has grouped them as follows:

   I. Emotional Gifts
       1 Corinthians 13:1, "Though I speak with the tongues . . ."

  II. Intellectual Gifts
       1 Corinthians 13:2a, "And though I have the gift of prophecy, . . . and mysteries, . . . and knowledge . . ."

 III. Practical Gifts
       1 Corinthians 13:2b, " . . . though I have all faith, so that I could remove mountains, . . ."

IV. Philanthropic, Sacrificial Gifts
   1 Corinthians 13:3, "though I bestow all my
   goods to feed the poor, . . . give my body to be
   burned, . . ."

Yet another scholar has divided the gifts into two
groups as follows:

I. Gifts Connected With the Ministry of the
   Word Apostleship, prophecy, discerning of
   spirits, teaching, etc.

II. Gifts Connected With Practical Uses
   Miracles, healings, rulings, helps, governments,
   etc.

Still another author divides the gifts into three all-
inclusive categories:

I. Gifts of Revelation
   Word of wisdom
   Word of knowledge
   Discerning of spirits

II. Gifts of Power
   Faith
   Working of miracles
   Healing

III. Gifts of Inspiration
   Prophecy
   Tongues
   Interpretation of tongues

Another commentator divides the gifts as follows:

I. Basic Ministries, Gifts of Edification
   Prophecy, teaching, etc.

II. Sign Gifts for Authentication
   Miracles, healings, tongues, etc.

Another astute student of the Bible groups the different gifts into two categories:

I. Natural Gifts

Capacities originally found in human nature, elevated, enlarged by the gifts of the Spirit, such as:

Teaching — capacity to impart knowledge
Healing — the physician's art
Helps — the work of deacons and church officers
Government — natural leadership

II. Supernatural Gifts
Prophecy
Miracles
Tongues

And finally, a seventh scholar categorized them as either continuing or transitory:

I. Eleven Permanent Gifts

For the building up of the body:
For the edification of the church (Eph. 4:12-15):
Apostles (in the original sense of one sent on a mission), prophets, evangelists, pastors, teachers, helps, administration, exhortation, giving, mercy, faith.

II. Five Temporary Gifts

Signs to substantiate, corroborate the message:
For unbelievers to authenticate the message (1 Cor. 14:22):
Miracles, healings, tongues, interpretation of tongues, discerning of spirits.

These seven groupings I have chosen as typical of so many others. Every commentator and every scholar will have his own individual approach to these charismatic phenomena. Before we begin our own discussion of these heavenly endowments poured out upon the churches, let me make several observations concerning them as they are presented in the Bible.

One striking, salient, yet deplorable fact about the

churches to whom the fullest, richest gifts were bestowed is this: the people who possessed these spiritual gifts (even the highest gift of prophecy) were by no means spiritually faultless. The gifts were mixed with human infirmity, and that sometime of the most reprehensible kind. These supernaturally gifted church members were not automatons, even though endowed by the Spirit. They carried with them all their human foibles and weaknesses. Inspiration is one thing, infallibility and sanctification yet another thing. The gifts possessed by the saints were subject to frequent misuse: disorder, vanity, false ambition, exalted self-esteem, overweening egotism, personal superiority. It is hard for the neophyte who is being introduced to the leadership of the church for the first time to understand this. But it is always tragically true and the sooner the initiate learns the hard lesson, the sooner he can continue in the love and admonition of the Lord. Some of the greatest saints have the most glaring faults. They all have feet of clay. None is perfect. Imperfections mar every great life with the exception only of that of the blessed Lord Jesus.

The churches themselves, made up of these imperfect people, also fall into every conceivable kind of error and heresy. False prophets and false spirits lead them astray. Leaders are dominated by personal motives. The entire body is sometimes off on a diverging tangent. Fanaticism often destroys the holiest and purest of the gifts. There must have been something of emotional cynicism that seized the church at Thessalonica to make Paul write to the congregation, "Despise not prophesyings" (1 Thess. 5:20). Because of these extreme weaknesses, Paul established rules of control over spiritual gifts and declared the need for subjection. In 1 Corinthians 14:29-32 he writes:

Let the prophets speak two or three, and let the other judge. If any thing be revealed to another that sitteth by, let the first hold his peace. For ye may all prophesy one by one, that all may learn, and all may be comforted. And the spirits of the prophets are subject to the prophets.

Even the prophet could be misled. His revelation or vision or message must be judged as to its truth by the other prophets. "The spirits of the prophets are subject to the prophets." In fact, so vital was it to the life of the infant church that the truth be unalloyed, that the Holy Spirit bestowed upon some of the members a charismatic gift called "discerning of spirits" (1 Cor. 12:10). John admonished the believers in 1 John 4:1, "Beloved, believe not every spirit, but try the spirits whether they are of God: because many false prophets are gone out into the world." So prone is the human heart to err and so misguided can be the human spirit, that the divine wisdom set selfguards in the churches to deliver us from the weaknesses of men.

Unity in Diversity

Let us note, also, the make-up of these New Testament churches. They are a unity in a multitudinous diversity. The members of the churches greatly differ, and most especially so in their gifts. Some things of the Spirit we all have in common. All of us have been regenerated by the Spirit. All of us have been baptized by the Spirit into the body of Christ. All of us are temples (in our bodies) of the Holy Spirit. All of us, insofar as we yield ourselves, are comforted, guided and helped by the Holy Spirit. But there the likeness ends. We all have differing gifts and differing degrees of the same gifts. Is this bad? No. It pleases God to make us to differ. We are all needed with our separate gifts to make the Church of Christ glorious.

Paul illustrates in 1 Corinthians 12:12-17 our unity in diversity by the human body. He writes in verses 14-20:

For the body is not one member, but many. If the foot shall say, Because I am not of the hand, I am not of the body; is it therefore not of the body? And if the ear shall say, Because I am not the eye, I am not of the body; is it therefore not of the body? If the whole body were an eye, where were the hearing? If the whole were hearing, where were the smelling? But now hath God set the members every one of them in the body, as it hath pleased him. And if they were all one member, where were the body? But now are they many members, yet but one body.

We all are needed. Every member of the church with his separate gift is necessary to the well-being of the whole.

John uses the world of creation to illustrate the manifold diversity of the sovereign will of God. He writes in John 1:1, 2: "In the beginning was the logos [the creative, activating principle], . . . All things were made by him [the creating Christ]; and without him was not any thing made that was made." Look around you. What kind of a world do you see? The great, living Spirit shows Himself under divers, even opposite, manifestations. But the law is one and the Spirit is one. Lead sinks and wood floats, but they are expressions of the one and the same creative Spirit. The difference between the spiritually-minded man and the materialistically-minded man is this: The materialist sees nothing but an infinite collection of unconnected, unrelated facts, broken, distorted, fragmentary, disordered. He is the existential philosopher. For him, life, the world, existence, creation, have no meaning. It all came from nowhere. It is all going nowhere. It is an accidental concourse of meaningless atoms, signifying nothing. But to the spiritually-minded man, every created thing has a part in the divine purpose of God. All are parts to make up the ultimately perfect whole. As the spiritual man progresses in understanding, he sees the number of basic laws diminish until at last they all are reduced to one; namely, the one that lies beneath the innumerable phenomena of nature — the Spirit of God. All living unity is spiritual not physical; it is inward, not outward. The works of the Spirit of God ever are characterized by diversity, complexity, multifariousness; not sameness.

It is thus with us in the churches. Our unity is not that we are all alike in a dull, wearisome monotony. Our unity is not one of outward uniformity but one of inward motivation. We all are activated by the same living principle, the same quickening Spirit, the same animating vision. We all are moving toward the same holy end. We are like the vision of Ezekiel's first chapter. The prophet saw wheels, faces, rims, eyes, wheels within wheels, and each part differing from the other part. But all the parts moved together, activated by the same living principle, the same quickening Spirit. Ezekiel writes in 1:20, 21:

> Whithersoever the spirit was to go, they went, thither was their spirit to go; and the wheels were lifted up over against them: for the spirit of the living creature was in the wheels. When those went, these went; and when those stood, these stood; and when those were lifted up from the earth, the wheels were lifted up over against them: for the spirit of the living creature was in the wheels.

It is thus with the differing members of the church. We possess a unity, not like the pebbles on a beach — a lifeless identity of outward form with no cohesion between the parts, a dead shore on which nothing grows, where even the seaweed dies. Our oneness is like that of the living world, full of infinite diversities which are but expressions of the same living Spirit. The Holy Spirit bestows upon us different gifts. No two of us are alike, as no two leaves are alike, and as no two snowflakes are alike. But however we differ, we are all a part of the testimony of the one saving Spirit.

56

Each Gift of Each Member Is Vitally Needed

Again Paul emphasizes the contribution each member of the Church can make to the household of faith. All members are needed in the body of Christ. Each one has a special part to play without which the body is broken, enfeebled, destroyed. He writes in 1 Corinthians 12:21-26:

> And the eye cannot say unto the hand, I have no need of thee; nor again the head to the feet, I have no need of you. Nay, much more those members of the body, which seem to be more feeble, are necessary: And those members of the body, which we think to be less honourable, upon these we bestow more abundant honour; and our uncomely parts have more abundant comeliness. For our comely parts have no need: but God hath tempered the body together, having given more abundant honour to that part which lacked: That there should be no schism in the body; but that the members should have the same care one for another. And whether one member suffer, all the members suffer with it; or one member be honoured, all the members rejoice with it.

When one member is hurt or cut off, all the members are hurt and weakened. This is true even of the smallest member. I hardly know I have a little toe. I rarely think of it; I rarely look at it; I seldom notice it. It is there but I am hardly aware of it. That is, until something happens to it! Then I do believe I am all little toe! It throbs and aches and is in pain until I cannot sleep, or study, or do any work at all. Yet, what I may come to realize is so important: the health of my little toe, so nearly forgotten throughout the hours of the day, affects the health of the whole body. We all have a worthy contribution to make to the body of Christ, even our feeblest parts. Without these humblest members, the body is not complete.

For forty-eight years our church has conducted noonday, pre-Easter services in a downtown theater. My illustrious predecessor, Dr. George W. Truett, conducted them for twenty-five years and this is now the twenty-third year that I have preached through them. Long ago, when I had just come to be the new pastor of the church, and after I had finished delivering the message at one of those noonday services, I walked through the front lobby of the theater. There I was met by a little, old, stooped lady, dressed in an old-fashioned, black dress. She said to me: "I have been so eager to see my new pastor, but I am too old and sick to go to church. Since today was such a beautiful, warm day, a neighbor brought me downtown to attend this service in order that I might see you. I wish I could help you but I am too old, too sick, and too poor. All I can do is pray for you." I put my arms around that stooped, little, old lady and said: "All you can do is pray! My sweet, little mother in Christ, that means more than anything else in the world. You speak as though it were so small. No. It is the greatest help of all. God hear you as you call my name before the throne of grace and ask His power to fall upon me." One of the gifts 1 Corinthians 12:9 is the gift of faith, the ability to claim the promises of God, to lay hold on the horns of the altar and intercede until victory comes. We could never have too many members like that frail, little lady who could only pray. "Nay," as Paul wrote, "much more those members of the body, which seem to be more feeble, are necessary" (1 Cor. 12:22). God has a place for us all, a gift for us all, in the assembly of the faithful.

Chapter 8

Charismatic Gifts for the Great Commission

Ephesians 4

¹¹ And he gave some, apostles; and some, prophets; and some, evangelists; and some, pastors and teachers.

In this passage in Ephesians 4:11 there are named in order of importance five ministering gifts of Christ to His church. The first one, "apostles," is named also in the list of Spirit gifts in 1 Corinthians 12:28. The second one, "prophets," is named also in the list of Spirit gifts in Romans 12:6 and in 1 Corinthians 12: 10 as well as in 1 Corinthians 12:28. It is the only one listed in all four places where Spirit gifts are named. The third one, "evangelists," is named only here. The fourth one, "pastors," is also named only here. The fifth one, "teachers," is listed in two other places; namely, in Romans 12:7 and in 1 Corinthians 12:28.

These five gifts to the churches named in Ephesians 4:11 are basic to the evangelization of the world and to the ministry of the Word. Without them the churches would not be, and the body of Christ would have no existence. They are vital to the carrying out of the Great Commission in Matthew 28:19, 20. There we are told to disciple (*matheteuo*) all nations, to baptize (*baptizo*) our converts, and to teach them (*didasko*) the words and the commandments of the Lord. For that tremendous assignment of conquest and training, the triune God in whose name we are baptized bestows five gifts upon His churches.

59

The Apostolic Gift

The first and foremost of all the endowments of the Spirit is that of apostleship. The word "apostle" *(apostolos)* was an ordinary, household Greek word meaning "messenger," "one sent forth." In Hebrews 3:1 our Saviour is called "the Apostle and High Priest of our profession" because He was "sent forth" from heaven to make atonement for our sins. From the equivalent Latin word of *missio* we gain our English word "missionary." The word *apostolos* is used in two ways in the New Testament: first, in a limited, technical sense, referring to an office; and second, in a general sense referring to a missionary.

The technical sense of the word *apostolos*, referring to an office, is used as a designation for the twelve apostles of Christ (Matt. 10:2; Luke 6:13; Acts 1:25, 26). We read in Luke 6:13, "And when it was day, he called unto him his disciples: and of them he chose twelve, whom also he named apostles." On special grounds the word was also used as a designation for Paul (Rom. 1:1; Gal. 1:1; 1 Cor. 9:1, 2; 2 Cor. 12:12). The word was probably also used to describe the sacred office held by James, the pastor of the church in Jerusalem and the Lord's brother (1 Cor. 15:7; Gal. 1:19). However the Lord will name them, there are always just twelve apostles, called "The Twelve" (Matt. 26: 20; Mark 14:17; Luke 22:14; Matt. 26:47; John 6:71, etc.). I believe that in the first chapter of Acts the disciples chose Mathias to be the apostle to take the place of the fallen Judas, but in the ninth chapter of Acts, God chose Saul of Tarsus. In any event, through time and eternity there are always just twelve apostles. Some day, according to Matthew 19:28 and Luke 22:29, 30, they will sit upon twelve thrones judging the twelve tribes of Israel. The Bride of Christ, the City of God, the New Jerusalem, is built upon twelve foundations, "and in them the names of the twelve apostles of the Lamb" (Rev. 21:14).

Most explicitly do the Scriptures avow that the apostles laid the foundation for the church. "And are built upon the foundation of the apostles and prophets, Jesus Christ himself being the chief corner stone" (Eph. 2:20). They laid the doctrinal foundation for the body of Christ (Acts 2:42). They laid the structural foundation for the temple of the Lord (Acts 1:15). They used the keys of the kingdom to open the doors to the Jews and to the Gentiles (Acts 2:9-11). They formed the link joining the Old Dispensation with the New. Through them is found unity and continuity in God's purpose of grace. Their roots were in the Old Testament but their ministry was in the New.

The twelve apostles have no successors. For one to be an apostle he had to be baptized by John the Baptist, had to be trained by Christ Himself, and had to be a personal eyewitness of the resurrected and glorified Lord (Acts 1:22). The group did not form a Sanhedrin or a great council. Like the delegates to a constitutional convention, when their work was done the office ceased. In the first chapter of Acts, the Twelve are prominently mentioned; thereafter, they are hardly referred to. After the doctrinal order of the church was committed to writing by inspiration of the Holy Spirit, the Scriptures became the authority for all faith and practice. The carrying out of the work of the Great Commission became the responsibility of all the members of the body of Christ to which the Holy Spirit gave superlative gifts. The last time the twelve apostles were together was in Acts 15 at the Jerusalem Conference. They were assembled there with the elders of the local church. Not Peter but James, the Lord's brother, presided. The whole membership of the church participated in the decision (Acts 15:22). After the Conference the Twelve were widely scattered and with a few exceptions are never heard of again. When they died the office ceased to exist. There are no more twelve apostles.

61

But there is another use in the word *apostolos* in which sense the Holy Spirit bestows the gift upon His churches today. In a general definition of the word it refers to the missionary who preaches Christ where He is not known, who gathers new converts together, and who organizes them into churches (compare Paul as he writes in Romans 15:20, 21, "Yea, so have I strived to preach the gospel, not where Christ was named . . ."). In this general sense, Andronicus and Junia are called "apostles" (Rom. 16:7). In this use of the word the messengers who accompany Titus in 2 Corinthians 8:23 are called "apostles." (The word translated "messengers" in the King James version is in the Greek "apostles."). In this sense Epaphroditus, in Philippians 2:25, is called an "apostle" (translated in the King James version "messenger"). In this sense the Holy Spirit anoints certain of His disciples today. On the mission field I have seen preachers of the Gospel who were endowed with the unusual gift of winning converts and founding churches in heathen, idolatrous communities. This is the continuing blessing of the Holy Spirit upon those who "preach the gospel where Christ is not named." They are first and foremost in the gift of God to the churches and ought to be thus honored and supported.

The Prophetic Gift

The second gift of the Spirit to the churches is that of "prophet." The Greek verb *propheteo* means to forthtell, to speak out concerning divine things. The noun form, *prophetes*, refers to one who has insight into divine things and who speaks them forth to others. The meaning of "foretelling," "prediction," in the word "prophet" is secondary and incidental. Only in medieval times did the word pass into the English language in the sense of prediction. A "prophet" in the Bible is always one who speaks out for God. The word is used in two ways in the New Testament:

first, in a limited, technical sense referring to an office; second, in a general sense referring to a gift of edification and inspiration.

There is a vast difference between the prophetic office and the gift of prophecy. This difference is carefully delineated in the Scriptures. When we think of the prophetic office, we think of Moses, Samuel, David, Elijah, and Isaiah of the Old Testament. In the New Testament we think of Paul, Agabus, Judas and Silas (Acts 11:27, 28; 15:32; 21:10, 11). Yet, the Scriptures state in Acts 19:6 that these new converts, these raw recruits in Ephesus, did prophesy. Are they to be numbered with Moses, Isaiah and Paul? No. There is a difference between the prophetic office and the gift of prophecy. The difference is again seen in the passage in Acts 21:9, 10. There the four virgin daughters of Philip the Evangelist are described as "prophetesses," but Agabus the prophet is set apart in deliberate contradistinction. Those who prophesy are prophets, but not in the grand, limited, technical sense of Moses, Isaiah and Paul. In the listings of the gifts of God to the churches, the "prophet" is second only to the "apostle" in Ephesians 4:11. But in the list in 1 Corinthians 12:28 the gift of prophecy comes down in the enumeration in importance. If the prophetic gift qualified for the prophetic office there would have been a correspondence in the two listings. In 1 Corinthians 14:1 we are admonished to seek not an office (that of a prophet) but a gift (the gift of edification).

Before the writing of the New Testament, the office of "prophet" was a vital one. The prophet told the infant church what it should do, believe and teach. Hence, Ephesians 2:20 reads, "And are built upon the foundation of the apostles and prophets, Jesus Christ himself being the chief corner stone." This necessitated also the gift of discerning of spirits (1 Cor. 12: 10), for it was most needed to distinguish between

63

the true revelations from God and false revelations concerning His churches. "The spirits of the prophets are subject to the prophets" (1 Cor. 14:32). "Let the prophets speak two or three, and let the other judge" (1 Cor. 14:29). Prophesyings were not to be despised (1 Thess. 5:20) but their utterances were to be carefully judged (1 John 4:1; Rev. 2:2). When the New Testament was complete, the office of prophet ceased. It was no longer needed. Our appeal now is to the inspired, written Word, not to a man. There are no more revelations to be added to God's Holy Book.

But as with the word *apostolos*, so with the word *prophetes*; there is a general sense in which the gift of the Holy Spirit is poured out upon certain of to-day's believers. The gift of prophecy is the most prominently witnessed of all the Spirit gifts seen today. It is a gift to be desired by the church (1 Cor. 14: 1, 39). In 1 Corinthians 12 - 14 some form of the word occurs twenty-two times. The purpose of the gift is seen in 1 Corinthians 14:3: "But he that prophesieth speaketh unto men to edification and exhortation, and comfort"; in 1 Corinthians 14:24, 25: "But if all prophesy, and there come in one that believeth not, or one unlearned, he is convicted of all, he is judged of all"; and in 1 Corinthians 14:31: "For ye may all prophesy one by one, that all may learn, and all may be comforted." The Spirit gift of prophecy is bestowed upon the churches for edification, exhortation, comfort, conversion of the lost, and teaching of the unlearned. It should be the gift most commonly exercised in the assemblies of Christ (1 Cor. 14:3, 24, 31). A preacher who gives forth the message of God in the wisdom and power of the Holy Spirit has the gift of prophecy (1 Peter 4:10, 11; 1 Cor. 2:1-16). Prophecy is Spirit-inspired utterance. An inspired preacher was the first gift of the Spirit manifested in the church at Pentecost. He is God's man for the delivering of God's message to a lost world. We must never forget Revelation 19:10, "For the testimony of Jesus is the spirit of prophecy."

The Evangelistic Gift

The third gift of the Lord to His people is that of "evangelist." The Greek verb *evaggelizo* means to bring good tidings. The noun form of the word, *evaggelistes*, refers to the messenger of good news. The word "evangelist" is used three times in the New Testament. Philip one of the seven ordained in Acts 6:5, is called "the evangelist" in Acts 21:8. Paul uses the word in 2 Timothy 4:5 when he admonishes Timothy, the pastor of the church at Ephesus, to "do the work of an evangelist." The third time the word is used is here in Ephesians 4:11 in the gifts of God to His churches.

The word *evaggelistes* involves two ideas. First, it refers to the kind of message preached, the good news of salvation. Second, it refers to the places in which the message is preached, which places are defined in the Scriptures as "scattered abroad." The different "scattered abroad" places can be seen in the itinerate ministry of Philip. The gift of the evangelist is a distinct gift which few men possess in superlative degree, but when it is found, it is the third of all the gifts of the Holy Spirit, preceded only by the gifts of apostleship and prophecy. The famous evangelists through the years have been men so greatly used of God to bless the world. We need them desperately. May God grant that the gift with increased frequency and meaning may fall upon our preachers today.

The Pastoral Gift

Strangely enough, the word "pastor," the fourth gift of the Lord to the churches, is used only once in the entire New Testament, here in Ephesians 4:11. The Greek word is *poimen*, meaning "shepherd." The New Testament uses three titles to describe the same office in the Church: *episcopos*, meaning "overseer," *presbuteros*, meaning "elder," and *poimen*, meaning "shepherd." The word "bishop" (*episcopos*) refers to the work of the pastor. The word "elder" (*presbuteros*) refers to the dignity and rank of his position. The word "shepherd," "pastor," (*poimen*) refers to his relationship to the flock. All three words are referred to in Acts 20:17, 18. The qualifications of a pastor are written in 1 Timothy 3:1-7; Titus 1:5-9, and in 1 Peter 5:1-4. Pastors are to be obeyed and to be held in high honor (Heb. 13:17). Those who are worthy are to be held in double honor (1 Tim. 5:17). This is the gift of the Spirit that is most preciously cherished by the people of Christ. A worthy pastor is a true benediction from heaven.

The Teaching Gift

The fifth of the spirit gifts to the assemblies of Christ is that of "teachers," listed in three of the categories named by the Apostle Paul (Rom. 12:7; 1 Cor. 12:28; Eph. 4:11). It is the God-given ability to explain the Holy Word, especially to newborn babes in Christ. It is a gift so greatly needed in the churches. The Great Commission is carried out through two main channels of work: preaching, which is directed to the will; and teaching, which is directed to the understanding. With these two gifts in powerful evidence, any people can make an impact for Christ upon a pagan world. Lord, give them to us in increasing meaning and power!

Chapter 9

Precious Ministering Gifts of the Spirit

1 Corinthians 12

7 But the manifestation of the Spirit is given to every man to profit withal.

8 For to one is given by the Spirit the word of wisdom; to another the word of knowledge by the same Spirit;

9 To another faith by the same Spirit; to another the gifts of healing by the same Spirit;

10 To another the working of miracles; to another prophecy; to another discerning of spirits; to another divers kinds of tongues; to another the interpretation of tongues.

Romans 12

6 Having then gifts differing according to the grace that is given to us, whether prophecy, let us prophesy according to the proportion of faith;

7 Or ministry, let us wait on our ministering: or he that teacheth, on teaching:

8 Or he that exhorteth, on exhortation; he that giveth, let him do it with simplicity; he that ruleth, with diligence: he that sheweth mercy, with cheerfulness.

There is literally a profusion of rich gifts of the Holy Spirit to make sweet and noble the work of the Church. They are precious endowments that bless the congregations of the Lord and fit us for godly service. We who belong to the household of faith are to be like our Saviour who came, "not to be ministered unto, but to minister" (Matt. 20:28). In spirit and in attitude we are to be like Him who said: "If I then, your Lord and Master, have washed your feet; ye also ought to wash one another's feet. For I have given you an example, that ye should do as I have done unto you" (John 13:14, 15). These precious ministering gifts I have grouped under four headings: first, Enlightenment of Mind; second, Sympathy of Heart; third, Practical Administration; fourth, Sublimity of Faith.

The Gifts of Wisdom and of Knowledge

In 1 Corinthians 12:8 the Apostle Paul names the first two gifts of the Spirit as "the word of wisdom" and "the word of knowledge." These have to do with the mind, the understanding, when it is consecrated to God. The first of the nine endowments listed in the passage is "the word of wisdom," (Greek, *logos sophias*). The gift has to do with the making known, to the people of the Lord, God's plan and purpose for His Church. It has to do with the spiritual principles that govern God's elective choices for us. It presents the deep, spiritual truths that lie back of God's will for our lives. It reveals to us what to believe and how to do in the wisdom of God. In 1 Corinthians 12:32 one of the twelve tribes is described in these words, "the children of Issachar, which were men that had understanding of the times, to know what Israel ought to do." They had the gift of wisdom. In Acts 5:38, 39 the famous Rabbi Gamaliel said, concerning the persecution that rose against the first Christian disciples: "And now I say unto you, Refrain from these men, and let them alone; for if this counsel or this work be of men, it will come to nought: But if it be of God, ye cannot overthrow it; lest haply ye be found even to fight against God." He had the gift of wisdom. Elevated, purified, the gift is bestowed in sublime proportions upon the followers of Christ. The apostles were led by the spirit of wisdom to create the diaconate

68

in order that the Church may be properly cared for (Acts 6:1-7). Stephen, one of the seven, was so filled with power that his opponents "were not able to resist the wisdom and the spirit by which he spake" (Acts 6:9, 10). Peter was wondrously used of God to explain to the Church at Jerusalem the opening of the door of conversion to the Gentiles (Acts 11:1-18). James, pastor of the Church at Jerusalem, presided over the Jerusalem Conference in Acts 15 and delivered the final pronouncement concerning the law and the Gospel. This is the gift of "the word of wisdom," knowing and explaining the mind and the purposes of God for our lives.

Second only to "the word of wisdom" is the gift of "the word of knowledge," (Greek, *logos gnoseos*). This is the gift of appraisal and of judgment concerning things as they are. It is the ability to grasp the truth about a present situation: seeing, knowing, understanding, as the Holy Spirit sees, knows and understands. In 2 Kings 5:20-27 is recounted the remarkable story of the prophet Elisha and his servant Gehazi. As the prophet recounted the perfidy of the greedy Gehazi, he said: "Went not mine heart with thee, when the man turned again from his chariot to meet thee?" (verse 26). This is the word of knowledge. In the story of the life of the same prophet, it is written that the king of Syria called his staff of ministers together to seek out the traitor among them, for the very thoughts of the monarch were immediately known to his enemies in Israel. The king despairingly asked: "Will ye not shew me which of us is for the king of Israel?" The answer came swift and certain: "And one of his servants said, None, my lord, O king: but Elisha, the prophet that is in Israel, telleth the king of Israel the words that thou speakest in thy bedchamber" (2 Kings 6:8-12). This is the word of knowledge. In the New Testament the gift is most meaningfully and gloriously illustrated. When Simon Peter said to our Lord Jesus in Matthew 16:16, "Thou art the Christ, the Son of the living God," the Saviour replied to His chief apostle, "Blessed art thou, Simon Barjona: for flesh and blood hath not revealed it unto thee, but my Father which is in heaven." The word of knowledge is seen in this heavenly recognition. An earthly recognition is succinctly illustrated in the conversation of our Lord with the woman of Samaria. The interchange of words goes like this:

> Jesus saith unto her, Go, call thy husband, and come hither. The woman answered and said, I have no husband. Jesus said unto her, Thou hast well said, I have no husband: For thou hast had five husbands; and he whom thou now hast is not thy husband: in that saidst thou truly (John 4:16-18).

This reminds me of a story I read told by the noble London preacher, F. B. Meyer. Speaking in the Free Assembly Hall in Edinburgh, he said: "There is a man here who owes his employer three pounds and eighteen shillings. Until that sum is repaid, that young man will never have peace with God." The preacher did not know of whom he was speaking. He said the words through "a gift of knowledge." Soon a young man made an appointment to see the preacher. When they were together the youth said, "Do you know me?" The preacher answered, "No, I never saw you before." The young employee answered, "In your sermon you described exactly what I did. My soul has been troubled ever since. Already there is a letter in the mail with a check returning the money."

It was with this gift of knowledge that Peter revealed the covetous corruption in the Jerusalem church, recorded in Acts 5:3. It was with this gift of knowledge that John wrote of the Seven Churches of Asia in Revelation 2, 3. It is with this gift of knowledge that God's leaders in the churches today come to know in right judgment and appraisal the moral, sound, doctrinal, and organizational situation that blesses the work of our Lord.

The Gift of Sympathy of Heart

The next grouping of these precious gifts of the Spirit I have chosen to call "Sympathy of Heart." Several of the gifts have to do with those precious mysteries that comfort and encourage God's people. Three of them are named in the list in Romans 12: 6-8. One is the gift of mercy. Paul writes of it in these words, *ho eleon en hilarotati*, "he that showeth mercy, with cheerfulness." The Greek word *eleos* means "mercy," "pity," especially in the presence of human misery such as is so often seen among the poor, the sad, the afflicted, the widows and the orphans. The New Testament Greek word for alms *eleemosune*, is built upon the basic word *eleos* and is the origin of our English word "eleemosynary," an adjective to describe charitable institutions and donations. The gift of mercy is the gift to sympathize with and to suffer alongside those who fall into grievous affliction. God so sympathizes with us. There is a divine pity in God. Isaiah 63:9 reads: "In all their affliction he was afflicted, and the angel of his presence saved them: in his love and in his pity he redeemed them; and he bare them, and carried them all the days of old." Psalm 103:13, 14 says: "Like as a father pitieth his children, so the LORD pitieth them that fear him. For he knoweth our frame; he remembereth that we are dust." This is a gift like the heart of our heavenly Father, the ability to sympathize with another. There was a little girl who came home from school and told her mother about her playmate whose mother had died and who was so sad. The mother asked her child, "And what did you say, dear?" The child replied: "I did not say anything. I just went over to her desk, sat down by her side, and cried with her." Notice that the one possessing the gift is not to feel himself burdened with it, as though he were weighted with all the woe of the world. He is, rather, to minister in the assurance of God's victorious mercies. He is to be "joyous," "cheerful," (Greek, *hilaros*) over his deeds of compassion.

Another like gift Paul names in Romans 12:8 with these words, "he that exhorteth on exhortation," (Greek, *ho parakalon en te paraklesei*). The Greek verb *parakaleo* means "to call alongside," "to comfort," "to encourage." The noun form, *paraklesis*, means "consolation," "comfort," "encouragement." From that Greek word comes the word "paraclete," used as a title for the Holy Spirit in John 14:16, 26, and as a title for Christ in 1 John 2:1 (translated "advocate" in the King James version). This is the gift of "encouragement," "strengthening" so desperately needed by so many of the members of Christ's body. God does not forget us in our human frailty.

Yet another precious ministry that Paul names in Romans 12:8 he describes with these words, "He that giveth, let him do it with simplicity," (Greek, *ho metadidous en baploteti*). The Greek verb *metadidomi* means "to share with," "to impart." The Greek noun *baplotes* means "simplicity," "sincerity," "purity." This gift refers to a material ministry manifesting the love of Christ, a giving, not by sentiment or by emotions, but by the wisdom of the Spirit of God. I sometimes think it could describe the man who is endowed with the ability to make money and who uses his gift to bless the work of God in the churches.

The Gifts of Practical Administration

In another group of gifts Paul describes those of practical administration. In Romans 12:8 he speaks of one in these words, "he that ruleth with diligence," (Greek, *ho proistamenos en spoude*). The Greek verb *proistemi* means "to stand before," "to preside over," "to rule." The Greek word *spoude* means "speed," "haste," "diligence," and finally "earnestness." The man who presides over the congregation of the Lord is to be deeply sensitive to the needs of the group

72

and is to be diligently earnest in his response to them. In 1 Corinthians 12:28 Paul refers to this gift as one of "government," "administration," (Greek *kubarnesis*). A "kubernetes" is a steersman, a pilot (compare Acts 27:11; Rev. 18:17). The possessor of this gift is one who has the ability to guide the Church through all the fortunes and vicissitudes of daily life, maintaining order and holding the congregation to its heavenly assignment. According to 1 Timothy 5:17, the gift was entrusted to the pastor (the elder, the bishop) of the Church.

Another ministry gift of administration Paul describes in Romans 12:7 with these words, "ministry, let us wait on our ministering," (Greek, *diakonian en te diakonia*). A servant, in the Greek language, is called a *diakonos*, a "deacon." In 1 Corinthians 12:28 Paul refers to this gift under the word *antilepseis* (a word used only here in the New Testament). The word comes from the verb *antilambano*, which means "to take hold of," "to share in," to "help." The recipients of that gift are men who are able to assist the pastor in his work of guiding the welfare and destiny of the congregation. Happy is the pastor who has these God-appointed and God-blessed deacons.

The Gift of Faith

As we have spoken of the gifts of the Spirit that pertain to Enlightenment of Mind, Sympathy of Heart, and Practical Administration, we now discuss one that pertains to Sublimity of Faith. In the list of the nine gifts in 1 Corinthians 12:8-10, Paul names the third one as "faith," (Greek, *pistis*, meaning "trust," "belief," "faith"). There are three uses of the word *pistis*, "faith," in Scripture. One meaning refers to natural faith, mental recognition, and assent. James 2:19 describes the devils as believing the facts of the Gospel and trembling before them. Another meaning of *pistis* refers to saving faith, the committal of our souls to

73

Christ as Paul describes in 2 Timothy 1:12. A third meaning of the word refers to the gift of faith, power to lay hold on God's promises for results beyond our own ability to achieve. This gift of faith is so wondrously illustrated in the Bible. Hebrews 11:17-19 describes the faithful Abraham who believed that God would raise his son Isaac from the dead if the lad were slain in obedience to the commandment of the Lord.

> By faith Abraham, when he was tried, offered up Isaac: and he that had received the promises offered up his only begotten son, Of whom it was said, That in Isaac shall thy seed be called: Accounting that God was able to raise him up, even from the dead; from whence also he received him in a figure (Hebrews 11:17-19).

Witness the faith of Elijah, in 1 Kings 17:8-16, who believed that God would take care of both him and the widow's household through the years of the terrible drought. "The barrel of meal shall not waste, neither shall the cruse of oil fail, until the day that the Lord sendeth rain upon the earth." George Muller, by prayer and faith alone, sustained his orphanage in Bristol, England, for a generation. He once said, "It pleased the Lord to give me something like a gift of faith so that unconditionally I could ask and look for an answer." This man of prayer never asked another human being for any need of food, clothing, provisions. He only asked God and God answered abundantly, triumphantly. From paradise in Eden to Patmos in Revelation, this gift of faith marks the trail of the company of the blessed, the heaven-bound saints of God. No wonder the faith chapter, Hebrews 11, sounds like a roll call of God's heroes! The gift of faith was and is their sublimest endowment.

Chapter 10

The Gift of Miracles

1 Corinthians 12

⁷ But the manifestation of the Spirit is given to every man to profit withal.

⁸ For to one is given by the Spirit the word of wisdom; to another the word of knowledge by the same Spirit;

⁹ To another faith by the same Spirit; to another the gifts of healing by the same Spirit;

¹⁰ To another the working of miracles; to another prophecy; to another discerning of spirits; to another divers kinds of tongues; to another the interpretation of tongues:

¹¹ But all these worketh that one and the self-same Spirit, dividing to every man severally as he will.

Three times the charismatic gift of miracles is named in the twelfth chapter of 1 Corinthians; namely, in verses 10, 28, and 29. Three Greek words are used in the New Testament for "miracle"; namely, *semeion*, *tera*, and *dunamis*. *Semeion* is a miracle as a sign authenticating the divine mission of the doer. It is translated "sign." *Tera* is a miracle as a wonderful thing, named for the effect of astonishment it has on the beholder. It is translated "wonder." *Dunamis* is a miracle as an exhibition of divine power. It is translated "miracle" (as here in 1 Cor. 12:10, 28, 29), as a "mighty deed" (2 Cor. 12:12). All three words are used in such passages as Acts 2:22; 2 Corinthians 12:12; Hebrews 2:4.

A miracle is an interruption, an intervention, in the system of nature as we know it. It is a temporary

75

suspension of the laws that govern this world as we commonly observe them. A miracle is "supernatural," above the "natural." The virgin birth of our Lord Jesus Christ is a "miracle." There is no other way to explain the birth of Christ as one without a human father except as a sovereign act of God suspending the laws of nature. Sometimes we use the word "miracle" in a figurative sense. We say "a sunset is a miracle of beauty and loveliness," or, "a Christian is a miracle of grace," or, "a mother is a miracle of patience and self-sacrifice." But this use of the word is not in the same sense as turning common dust into insects (Moses), or dividing a stream by the sweep of a mantle (Elijah and Elisha), or feeding five thousand with a few loaves and fishes (Jesus). To turn water into wine through the processes of nature is one thing; to turn water into wine by fiat, as a sovereign act apart from the processes of nature, is another thing. The latter is truly a "miracle."

The Astonishing Gift of Miracles

The gift of miracles is an astonishing gift. In the list of charismata in 1 Corinthians 12:8-10, of the nine gifts named, that of "healing" is fourth and that of "miracles" is fifth. The gift of healing is a specific category within the larger gift of miracles. Miracles that are not bodily healings are illustrated in the fish with the shekel in its mouth, caught by Simon Peter at the direction of the Lord Jesus (Matt. 17:24-27), Jesus walking on the water (Matt. 14:25-33), Peter being liberated from Herod's prison with the iron gate opening of itself (Acts 9:36-42), and Paul calling down blindness on Elymas, the sorcerer in the court of Sergius Paulus (Acts 13:8-11).

The gift of miracles was not for show or for entertainment. Miracles in the Bible were never performed to be spectacular. They were never presented in a Circus Maximus to attract attention to the doer. In the second temptation (Matt. 4:5-7) Jesus pointedly refused to hurl Himself down from the pinnacle of the temple in order to be lavishly applauded by the people for His deliverance in so great a feat. When the Jews required of the Saviour a sign (Matt. 12:38-40), He refused to accommodate their empty curiosity with anything but a verbal denunciation of their hard hearts (Matt. 12:41, 42). The same reaction was witnessed in our Lord when He was brought to trial before Herod Antipas (Luke 23:5-11). The Scriptures state that "when Herod saw Jesus, he was exceeding glad . . . because he hoped to have seen some miracle done by him" (verse 8). When the Lord not only refused to work a cheap miracle for the monarch's entertainment but also refused even to answer him a word, Herod mocked Him and returned Him in contempt to Pontius Pilate. Never for ostentation was any miracle wrought, and for the most part the miracles of our Lord and of the apostles were works of compassion and mercy.

It is most noticeable that very few converts were won by "signs and wonders and miracles." After the feeding of the five thousand on the eastern side of the Galilean sea, Jesus left and made His way in a boat to Capernaum. The multitudes followed Him, walking to the city around the north end of the lake. When they found Him in Capernaum they were greeted with the announcement that they sought the Saviour not because they had seen in Him the presence of God but because "they did eat of the loaves and were filled" (John 6:26). When Jesus proceeded to preach to them a sermon on the bread of life, beginning with the words, "labor not for the meat which perisheth, but for the meat which endureth unto everlasting life" (verse 27), they were offended in Him and walked no more with Him (verse 66). The miracle of the feeding of the five thousand did not convert one life, not one. The same effect of the wonder-working life

77

of our Lord can be seen in the reaction of the Jewish rulers to Jesus. They finally, in desperation, attributed His astonishing power to Satan and furthermore set about to have Him removed from the earth. His restoration of life to the four-day dead Lazarus in Bethany was the climax that sealed His fate. Instead of the leaders' obdurate spirits softening and their hard hearts repenting, they gathered together the Sanhedrin to find formal means of putting Him to death (John 11: 47-53).

The sterile fruitlessness of conversion by miracles is dramatically emphasized by Jesus in His teaching. The story of Dives and Lazarus in the life beyond the grave is unforgettable. In torment Dives pleaded with father Abraham to send back to this earth Lazarus that the rich man's five brothers may be warned of hell and may thereby repent and be saved (Luke 16:19-31). Abraham replied, "They have the Bible (Moses and the prophets); let them hear them." To this the rich man responded, "Nay, father Abraham: but if the miracle of one raised from the dead could be seen by them and if that dead man's pleas for repentance and faith could be heard by them, they would turn and be saved." Abraham from heaven closed the conversation with these words: "If they heed not the appeal of the Word of God, neither will be persuaded though one rose from the dead." Miracles do not bring conversion, even the astonishing wonder of one raised from the grave. Thus said and thus taught the Lord Jesus.

The teaching and example of the Master concerning the effect of miracles on the unrepentant is corroborated in the experience of the apostles. In Acts 14: 8-18 the story is recounted of the reception of Paul and Barnabas as gods by the city of Lystra when the citizens saw Paul heal a man crippled all the days of his life. The narrative seemingly is about to present a glorious revival of salvation wrought by the convicting effect of one wondrous healing. But the story continues in verse 19 with these succinct words, "having stoned Paul, [they] drew him out of the city, supposing he had been dead." How empty and barren of results is conversion by miracle! When Paul healed the demented, spirit-possessed girl of Philippi (Acts 16:12- 24), we would have thought the whole populace would have rejoiced in so great a deliverance and that the Apostle would have received his greatest ovation. Instead, he and his companion, Silas, were brutally beaten because of the miracle and, furthermore, were placed in stocks and chains in the deepest part of the dungeon. The simple truth is that no saving faith is achieved by the miraculous. Nor did the apostles ever seek to evangelize through signs and wonders. They relied entirely upon the convicting, regenerating power of the Holy Spirit for their converts, the same as do we and the same God instructed from the beginning. No miracles are recorded in the Book of Acts as Luke recounts the founding of the churches in Pisidian Antioch, Derbe, Thessalonica, Berea, Athens, Corinth, and other places. We are saved by God not by miracle.

The Purpose of Miracles

What, then, is the purpose of the miraculous? Miracles are for introduction, for authentication, for corroboration, for substantiation. There have been times in the economy of God when they were mightly needed to introduce a new life, a new dispensation. They bore a special testimony at the beginning of each new age. The creation story (Gen. 1 - 3) is filled with miracles. The introduction of the law through Moses is filled with miracles. The revival under Elijah and Elisha, in the dark days of apostasy when it seemed that worship of the true God would die from the earth, is filled with miracles. The introduction of the Christian era, under Jesus and the apostles, is filled with miracles. The consummation of the age re-

79

counted in the Apocalypse is filled with miracles. But outside of these introductory eras they are rarely seen and hardly found. For example, they are much in evidence in the first part of the Book of Acts (cf. Acts 2:43). Then they become less and less common until in the latter part of the Book of Acts they are rarely mentioned.

No one could read Hebrews 2:3, 4 without astonishment. Look at the passage closely and carefully: "How shall we escape, if we neglect so great salvation; which at the first began to be spoken by the Lord, and was confirmed unto us by them that heard him; God also bearing them witness, both with signs and wonders, and with divers miracles, and gifts of the Holy Ghost, according to his own will?" (Hebrews 2: 3, 4). Whoever wrote the Book of Hebrews (and I think it was written by the eloquent Alexandrian orator, Apollos) belonged to the second generation of Christians. The author had not seen the Lord nor had he heard the message of the Gospel from the lips of the Saviour. He had heard it from those who had seen the Lord, second hand, second generation. But most important for us in our understanding of the gift of miracles, he had not seen the confirmation of "signs and wonders and divers miracles." Even in his second generation these had died out. The message was not confirmed to him by these miraculous signs; rather, the message was confirmed to *them* (the Apostles and the personal witnesses) by those miraculous authentications. He had heard the report of the miracles; he had not seen them himself.

The dying out of the gift of miracles is most reasonable and obvious. When they served their purpose, they ceased to be. They were needed no longer. Moses, going down into Egypt's land, was armed with three wondrous miracles for introduction: the rod into a serpent, the leprous hand cleansed, the water turned into blood (Exod. 4:1-9). Jesus authenticated His claim

80

to forgive sins (the prerogative of deity alone) by the miracle of raising the palsied man to strength and health (Mark 2:7-12). Paul confirmed his apostleship with "the signs of an apostle" (2 Cor. 12:12, "Truly the signs of an apostle were wrought among you in all patience, in signs and wonders, and mighty deeds," cf. Rom. 15:18, 19; Acts 19:11, 12). The two witnesses from heaven are fortified in the tragic days of the Great Tribulation with the power to do miracles.

> And I will give power unto my two witnesses, and they shall prophesy a thousand two hundred and threescore days, clothed in sackcloth. These are the two olive trees, and the two candlesticks standing before the God of the earth. And if any man will hurt them, fire proceedeth out of their mouth, and devoureth their enemies: and if any man will hurt them, he must in this manner be killed. These have power to shut heaven, that it rain not in the days of their prophecy: and have power over waters to turn them to blood, and to smite the earth with all plagues, as often as they will. And when they shall have finished their testimony, the beast that ascendeth out of the bottomless pit shall make war against them, and shall overcome them, and kill them (Rev. 11:3-7).

When the need for the sign ceased, the sign was no longer given.

The Church is built upon the foundation of the apostles and the prophets (New Testament inspired men who told the infant church what to do and what to believe). These apostles and prophets were accredited by signs and wonders and mighty works. After the foundation was laid, the office ceased. There were no more prophetic offices upon which the church is built. The prophets' utterances of wisdom and revelation are written down forever in the pages of the New Testament. There are no more apostolic offices upon which the church is founded. The apostles' message from heaven is forever contained in the inspired books of the New Testament. Look at the number of foundations undergirding the Bride of Christ (the church) in the New Jerusalem. They number twelve and twelve alone. The office of apostle is held by twelve men and twelve only. (As I have suggested already, the disciples at Jerusalem chose Matthias to take the office vacated by Judas Iscariot; I believe God chose Saul of Tarsus, Paul, to fill it.) In the foundation of the city are written the name of the twelve apostles of the Lamb. Upon them the church is built (Eph. 2:20). To these apostles in their sacred office (as to the infant church in its beginning) the gift of miracles was bestowed. The gift was for introduction and authentication. Paul writes to the church at Corinth: "for in nothing am I behind the very chiefest apostles, though I be nothing. Truly the signs of an apostle were wrought among you in all patience, in signs, and wonders, and mighty deeds" (2 Cor. 12: 11, 12). Here plainly is seen the purpose of the *semeion*, the *tera*, and the *dunamis*. The miracle confirmed the calling of the apostle to his holy office. After the foundation of the church was laid, the apostolic office ceased, and the sign ceased. There was no more need for authentication. The Bible is complete and our appeal now is not to an apostle in his God-appointed office but to the infallible, inspired Word. The infant church, blessed with the gift of miracles, confirmed in its doctrine and practice by signs of approval from heaven, is now firmly founded and the need for the sign has ceased to exist. We have the Bible and that is enough.

As no one person has all the gifts of the Spirit, so it is possible that no one age has all the gifts. If every Christian does not possess every charismatic endowment, then it could be that every generation does not possess all the gifts. This is certainly true with regard to the sign gift of miracles.

The Gift of Miracles and
Our Miracle-Working God

There is a vast difference between the miracles of God sovereignly wrought and the *gift* of miracles sovereignly bestowed. God can, has, does work miracles throughout history; yesterday, today and forever. The sign of the presence of God is always the miraculous, whether in heaven above or on earth beneath. If it is of God, it is wondrously miraculous. But the *gift* of miracles is always temporary. There are times in the history of God's elective grace bestowed upon men when the period is filled with intense activity and the gift of miracles is the wonder of the age (cf. the days of Moses, of Elijah, of Peter and Paul). But there are also times when the program of God enters a great calm, such as the four hundred years of silence between the days of Malachi and the days of Matthew. The gift of miracles appears, then enters a state of quiescence, then reappears more startling than ever. We shall witness a mighty return of the gift of miracles during the last days described in the Book of Revelation.

Miracles of God are on every hand. They are recorded every day. The *gift* of miracles possessed by the saints may be temporary but miracles and the miracle-working God are with us forever. God does not change or evolve. His power and wisdom are this day what they were before the morning stars sang together.

> Thou, Lord, in the beginning hast laid the foundation of the earth; and the heavens are the works of thine hands: They shall perish; but thou remainest; and they shall wax old as doth a garment; And as a vesture shalt thou fold them up, and they shall be changed: but thou art the same, and thy years shall not fail (Heb. 1:10-12).

The fires that forged the strong bands of Orion are the same as those that were seen by Moses in the burning bush of Horeb; that Israel looked upon in the Shekinah glory above the tabernacle and the temple; that smote Ahibu in the day of judgment; that consumed the sacrifice and the altar and the very dirt of the ground upon the appeal of Elijah; that rose in amber flames before the rapt attention of Ezekiel; that sat in cloven tongues upon Peter and the apostles; that blinded the eyes of Saul of Tarsus on the road to Damascus; and the same as shall someday clothe our glorious returning Lord when He descends through the clouds of heaven. God does not change nor does His power to work miracles among men cease.

The Book of Acts has no formal conclusion. The story stops in the middle of the most interesting part. This is because the writing of the Book of Acts has not concluded. The story does not cease with the present chapter 28. It is plainly an unfinished volume. Other chapters are being added, chapters 29, 30, 31 and on and on until the consummation of the age and the intervention of the Lord Christ in human history. On mission fields and in a thousand places the wondrous, miraculous works of God are seen. But the *gift* of miracles is not bestowed upon the servants of the Lord with great frequency, and when it is, it is for a special purpose. It is not a permanent but a special, temporary gift. Our faith and our assurance are not dependent upon a sign or a wonder or a miracle, but upon the promise of the Word of God and the witness of the Holy Spirit in our hearts (Rom. 8:14-17). This is enough. If God gave me a vision of an angel or a light from heaven or a flaming bush that burned unconsumed, I would be ever so greatful. If I could work miracles by the gift of God, I would praise His name forever. But these gifts lie in His sovereign will. I do not need their authenticating, confirming testimony. I have the word of the Lord and that is enough. I ask for no sign beside.

Chapter 11

The Gifts of Healing

1 Corinthians 12

⁹ To another faith by the same Spirit; to another the gifts of healing by the same Spirit.

Three times Paul names this sign gift of healing (one of the four sign gifts: miracles, healing, tongues, and interpretation of tongues) in the twelfth chapter of 1 Corinthians. It is mentioned in verses 9, 28 and 30. In all three instances the plural is used, *charismata iamaton*, "gifts of healings." As there are different kinds of sicknesses (we can be sick in our bodies, we can be sick in our minds, we can be sick in our souls), so there are different kinds of healings.

The discussion of illness and healing touches all our lives, both in ourselves and in the circle of our family and friends. There is no one but who knows the heartache of illness, and illness can be so tragic. In my first pastorate a young deacon and his wife called me to their home to pray for their little two-year-old baby girl stricken with diphtheria. "Tell the Lord," they desperately said to me, "that we will do anything for Him, give Him all we have and are, if only He will spare our precious child." I earnestly sought for an answer. I did so with all my heart. But the child died. That pitiful story has been repeated throughout these many years of my ministry and continues to this present day. Last week I received this letter from the wife of a preacher who is pastor of one of our finest churches:

Dear Dr. Criswell:

My husband is sick here in a Shreveport hospital. There are no medical answers and the time is urgent. You have great faith and have seen physical and spiritual miracles. Please pray in Jesus' name for my husband's healing.

We are expecting this healing not because my husband is a preacher. He would say that he is the least of His children. We trust God for a miracle because of His love, mercy, power, and willingness to heal.

Thank you for praying. Any promise that you claim for his healing or any suggestions on prayer will be helpful. We want God to get glory to His name.

Very gratefully yours,

But within a few days the pastor died.

It Is Right to Turn to God for Healing

What of the appeal to God in the hours of illness? It is right, it is pre-eminently correct and Scriptural to turn to God for healing. Only God can heal. All healing is divine healing. There is no other kind. Man can operate, cut, saw, sew, prescribe, diagnose, but only God can heal. We have every Scriptural right to look to heaven for healing. We have the right because of who and what God is. His very name is "Jehovah Ropheca," "I am the Lord that healeth thee" (Exod. 15:26). We have the right because of the example and the ministry of our Saviour. "When the even was come, they brought unto him many that were possessed with devils: and he cast out the spirits with his word, and healed all that were sick: That it might be fulfilled which was spoken by Esaias the prophet, saying, Himself took our infirmities, and bare our sicknesses" (Matt. 8:16, 17). We have this right because of the Spirit's indwelling. "But if the Spirit of him that raised up Jesus from the dead dwell in you, he that raised up Christ from the dead shall also quicken your mortal bodies by his Spirit that dwelleth in you"

(Rom. 8:11). All three Persons of the Godhead are pledged to this remembrance of our infirmities in saving, healing grace.

God has healed in days past in answer to prayer. God healed Abimelech when Abraham prayed for him (Gen. 20:7). God healed Miriam when Moses prayed for her (Num. 12:14). God healed Hezekiah when the king turned his face to the wall and with bitter weeping asked God for length of days. "Then came the word of the LORD to Isaiah, saying, Go, and say to Hezekiah, Thus saith the LORD, the God of David thy father, I have heard thy prayer, I have seen thy tears: behold, I will add unto thy days fifteen years" (Isa. 38:4, 5). Jesus healed the leper who in faith prayed to Him, "Lord, if thou wilt, thou canst make me clean" (Matt. 8:2). Recently, at a men's and boys' dinner in the church I heard the testimony of "the strongest man in the world," a man who had won the title at a world Olympic meet. To my amazement he began his talk with a divine healing experience. When he was a little boy, four years of age, the doctors said he could not live. In keeping with the customs of the times, arrangements were made in the home for his casket to be brought to the house. But a godly grandfather brought his sorrow to a pastor who prayed to God for the life of the child. The lad was miraculously delivered. The next day he was well. Could this be so? Yes. A thousand times yes. God heals! His name is "Jehovah Ropheca." "I am the LORD that healeth thee."

Professional Divine Healers and Their Gifts of Healing

But professional divine healers, with their purported "gifts of healing" for money, are something else. As there is an all-significant distinction between the miracles of God and "the gift of miracles," so there is an all-significant distinction between God's healings

87

and "the gifts of healing." The gift is a sign gift for the purpose of corroboration, authentication, substantiation, and introduction while the gospel message was in its formative state, before the New Testament was written. The sign gift authenticated the messages as from God. This is seen in the life of Jesus.

> Ye men of Israel, hear these words; Jesus of Nazareth a man approved of God among you by miracles and wonders and signs, which God did by him in the midst of you, as ye yourselves also know (Acts 2:22).

> How God anointed Jesus of Nazareth with the Holy Ghost and with power: who went about doing good, and healing all that were oppressed of the devil; for God was with him (Acts 10:38).

This is seen in the life of the apostles.

> By stretching forth thine hand to heal; and that signs and wonders may be done by the name of thy holy child Jesus (Acts 4:30).

It is seen in the life of Paul.

> Truly the signs of an apostle were wrought among you in all patience, in signs, and wonders, and mighty deeds (2 Cor. 12:12).

It is emphatically seen in the letter to the Hebrews.

> How shall we escape, if we neglect so great salvation; which at the first began to be spoken by the Lord, and was confirmed unto us by them that heard him; God also bearing them witness, both with signs and wonders, and with divers miracles, and gifts of the Holy Ghost, according to his own will? (Heb. 2:3, 4).

When the Word with its authority was written, the appeal no longer is to the "signs of an apostle" as Paul presented in 2 Corinthians 12:12, but to the holy verses of the Holy Book. The sign is no longer needed nor is it necessary. In Joshua 5:11, 12, we are told:

> And they did eat of the old corn of the land on the morrow after the passover, unleavened cakes, and

parched corn in the selfsame day. And the manna ceased on the morrow after they had eaten of the old corn of the land; neither had the children of Israel manna any more; but they did eat of the fruit of the land of Canaan that year.

The miracle of the manna in the wilderness was no longer needed. They ate of the fruit of the land. So with us. The miraculous sign-gift is no longer needed. We have the living Word.

The modern increase of professional money-making divine healers is a phenomenal development in itself. From an article in a current magazine I copy these words: "In Britain alone the number of spirit healers belonging to the National Federation of Spiritual Healers is in the region of four thousand, and the number of people who claim to be spirit healers is increasing all over the world. Hundreds of thousands claim to have been cured by them. One of the healers, all his life, has been guided by a voice. He claims his healing power comes from God. He smokes cigars and does not go to church. He believes that God does not need the trappings of religion, and goes down to the pub [liquor bar] after a day's work. Yet, his reported healings are numerous and remarkable." Through the wee hours of the morning I stood in Father Divine's central "heaven" in Harlem, New York City, and heard dozens of adorations addressed to the little "God" by people who had in answer to prayers poured out to him been miraculously healed. Until he died, this "God" kept on healing by miracle and kept up the lavish estate in which he and his "wife" and angels lived.

Yesterday I received this letter: "Send a snapshot of yourself or of any loved one who is in need of prayer. We will lay our hands upon the picture and ask God to meet every need. Your generous gifts and faithful pledges are needed. Read God's Bible promises for your healing. As you vow, pay your vows to the Lord.

Surely every Bible believing Christian can vow to give a hundred dollars. Some can give a thousand. I will be looking for your letter [and I might add, for your money]. Yours in God's Miracle." What do you think of that? If a man had the gifts of healing, I doubt that he should use it for money. But how do these professional miracle workers succeed and continue? For the simple reason that eighty-five percent of all the sick will get well anyway, and to the other fifteen percent the divine healers can blandly and piously say, "You do not have the faith." It is a sure-fire racket, far more certain than betting on horses at the race tracks or playing the game tables at Las Vegas. If the odds are eighty-five percent in your favor, how can you lose? Anyone can announce himself as a divine healer and make big money if he knows how to go about it, with personality, publicity, showmanship, and all the other accoutrements and embellishments of the trade. But oh, thus to prey upon the miseries of people! If there are gifts of divine healing they ought to be employed in a hospital, up and down the corridors; not in a tent, up and down the aisles.

The Distressing Doctrines of Professional Divine Healers

Remembering our sick and sorrowing, I hear and read so many hurtful fallacies that bring grief and distress to the soul. Let me recount some of the things professional divine healers avow. They say that God wills that we never be sick; that we all be well; that all the sick be healed; that none ever be sick. But you are sick. Why? The doctrine brings anguish to the sensitive soul. Why was Timothy, Paul's son in the ministry, continuously sick? Why did not God heal him? Paul refers in 1 Timothy 5:23 to Timothy's "often infirmities." He was such a teetotaler that he would not take even a small amount of medicine spirits for his sick stomach. Paul had to plead with

90

him to do so. Yet Paul had the miraculous "gift of healing." In 2 Timothy 4:20 Paul writes to Timothy, the pastor of the church at Ephesus, that he left Trophimus at Miletum sick. This is Paul's last letter. He is writing from the Mamertime dungeon in Rome from which imprisonment he was delivered to the headsman or block on the Ostian Way. Paul would never be in Asia again. He would never see Trophimus again. Why did not Paul heal him or leave a miracle-working handkerchief or apron? Is it truly God's will that we never be sick? Plainly, the gifts of the Spirit are sovereignly bestowed (1 Cor. 12:7, 11). They do not work indiscriminately. Even the apostles were not able to heal promiscuously. Not when men desire to employ them are the gifts of the Spirit seen, but when the Holy Spirit Himself desires to further some work of God.

Professional faith healers say that Christ healed *all* who were sick. But you are sick. Why does He not heal you? Apparently, God does not love you. He has forgotten you. No. Not at all. The fault lies in the false doctrine. Christ no more healed all the sick than He raised all the dead. He raised three from the dead (the widow's son from Nain, the daughter of Jairus, and the brother of Mary and Martha) and possibly others (Matt. 11:5), but the vast host of the bodies of the saints He left in their graves awaiting the final resurrection day. It is most preciously true that as Jesus entered the villages and cities of Galilee and the countryside round about, He healed all the sick who were brought to Him (Matt. 9:35; 10:1; 12:15; 14:14; Luke 6:17-19). This very ministry with its gifts of healing set Him apart, for such a mercy is not usually given unto man. The sign designated Him as the Son of God; it was the prerogative of deity. But this is not the whole story. Read John 5:1-9. Bethesda's porches were filled with the sick, all of them believing in divine healing, and all of them waiting for the heavenly miracle. But how many did Jesus heal? One. Read Luke 5:15, 16. The Saviour whose endearing name is "the Lord moved with compassion" withdrew from the multitudes who were sick, and went into the wilderness to pray. Think of the sick in the world whom He did not heal! The miracles of Christ were not for the purpose of contravening the judgment of God upon this world, a sentence solemnly pronounced in Genesis 3:14-19. Our deliverance from that awesome sentence of death was wrought through the atonement on Calvary, but the full effects will be seen only at the end of the world. (For example, 1 Cor. 15:26 says, "The last enemy that shall be destroyed is death.") The miracles of Christ were for the purpose of identifying Him as Saviour of the world; they bore evidence of His deity, they proclaimed Him to be the Son of God, they formed the credentials of His Messiahship (Mark 2:7-12; Acts 2:22; 10:38; Isa. 53:4; Matt. 8:17). The miracles of Christ were not for ostentation or notoriety, but that we could know the heart of God, "moved with compassion and touched with the feeling of our infirmity" (Heb. 4:15; Matt. 9:36; Mark 1:4; 6:34; Luke 7:12, 13).

The professional divine leader preaches that the atonement of Christ included not only all our sins but also all our illnesses. Our sins are carried away in the death of Christ and also our infirmities (Isa. 53). They say since disease entered by sin, its true remedy must be found in the redemptive work of Christ. This is true, of course, and the whole system of sin, disease, and the works of the devil are to be destroyed by the manifestation of Christ (1 John 3:8). But you are a Christian and you still sin, living sometimes in the agony of Paul in Romans 7:24, "O wretched man that I am! who shall deliver me from the body of this death?" Why? For the simple reason that all the benefits of the atonement are not immediately realized. The curse is still upon creation (Rom. 8:22). The woman is still in travail in childbirth. The man still must live by the toil and sweat of hard labor. The body still falls into age and senility. The drag of sin and human weakness is still the despair of our better hopes (Rom. 7:15-24). Accepting Christ does not change that. We are saved but we still groan within ourselves waiting for the redemption of our bodies (Rom. 8:23). Forgiven, the spirit regenerated, we must still wait for the resurrection of the whole purchased possession at the final day of the Lord. Though saved and sanctified, we still are not glorified. We still know sin and weakness in this life.

Illness Not a Sign of Disobedience to God

The faith-healer-for-hire yet avows another thing. He says that illness is a sign of disobedience to God. "Get right with God, do God's will," he proclaims, "and you will be well." I read a tract the other day which concludes with these words: "I don't care how many times you have been prayed for, it is God's will that you have a well body. Friend of mine, will you obey God? When you make up your mind to obey God you will be healed." But you are sick. It must be, therefore, that you have sinned in disobedience to God. So you live through the agony of soul-searching to ascertain what sin of disobedience has brought on such a heavy illness. This whole interpretation is inhuman and unsupported by Scripture. Job's comforters (divine healers) steadfastly avowed that Job's terrible sickness was due to his terrible sins. Yet God said he was the best man in all the earth (Job 1:8; 4:7, 8). Daniel became ill because of the abundance of the revelations given to him (Dan. 8:26, 27; 10:15-17). Look at this passage in John 9:1-3):

> And as Jesus passed by, he saw a man which was blind from his birth. And his disciples asked him, saying, Master, who did sin, this man, or his parents, that he was born blind? Jesus answered, Neither

hath this man sinned, nor his parents: but that the works of God should be made manifest in him.

A like sentiment is expressed by our Lord concerning the terminal illness of Lazarus: "When Jesus heard that, he said, This sickness is not unto death, but for the glory of God, that the Son of God might be glorified thereby" (John 11:4).

Paul wrote in 2 Corinthians 4:16, "For which cause we faint not; but though our outward man perish, yet the inward man is renewed day by day." Though the body weakens and finally loses all its strength, yet the inward spirit is daily renewed by the mercies of God, a situation that would not be true if the weakness were due to the sinful disobedience. Epaphroditus became ill unto death "for the work of Christ" (Phil. 2:27-30). Whatever Paul's "thorn in the flesh" may have been, when he writes of it he uses the word "infirmities" (sicknesses). He says:

And lest I should be exalted above measure through the abundance of the revelations, there was given to me a thorn in the flesh, the messenger of Satan to buffet me, lest I should be exalted above measure. For this thing I besought the Lord thrice, that it might depart from me. And he said unto me, My grace is sufficient for thee: for my strength is made perfect in weakness. Most gladly therefore will I rather glory in my infirmities, that the power of Christ may rest in me. Therefore I take pleasure in infirmities, in reproaches, in necessities, in persecutions, in distresses for Christ's sake: for when I am weak, then am I strong (2 Cor. 12:7-10).

He had just written in the first part of the letter (2 Cor. 1:8-11) that in Asia he had been sick unto death, "we had the sentence of death in ourselves." Paul knew what it was to be repeatedly ill, desperately so, even unto death. Were these tragic bodily weaknesses and illnesses due to his sinful disobedience? No, no, no! God answered Paul's inquiry and prayer with these sublime words: "My grace is sufficient for thee: for my strength is made perfect in weakness." And Paul answered God's will with these incomparable words of dedication: "Most gladly therefore will I rather glory in my infirmities, that the power of Christ may rest upon me" (2 Cor. 12:9). And this may be God's will for us. If it is, may we answer as fully as did His servant, the Apostle Paul.

Chapter 12

Faith and Healing

James 5

[14] Is any sick among you? let him call for the elders of the church; and let them pray over him, anointing him with oil in the name of the Lord:

[15] And the prayer of faith shall save the sick, and the Lord shall raise him up; and if he have committed sins, they shall be forgiven him.

There is a Christian attitude toward illness. First, let us admit its reality. Let us be honest if we are Christians! There is a large cult in Christendom that denies the existence of disease. They avow that its presence is only in the mind. Ignore it in the mind, overcome it in thought, and it will cease to be. I was pastor one time in a college town. A professor of music in the institution belonged to that cult. Her devoted mother was a faithful member of our church. The mother fell down the steps in her home to the concrete basement floor. She hurt herself terribly. The daughter ran down to her mother, helped her up, saying: "Mother, you are not hurt! You are not hurt!" I went out to the house to see the dear mother. She was very heavy and the fall had broken her up. She was black and blue all over. But no doctors could be called. No ointments or medicines could be used. Her hurt was only in her mind! The cult pursues that same denial of reality even unto death. A couple I knew belonged to the group. The husband died and the poor, lonely wife was in deepest grief. But after a representative of the cult called upon her, she acted as if she were getting ready for a birthday party, not a funeral. She was all smiles, gaiety and laughter. "For," she said, "my husband is not dead; death is only in the mind." But that casket and that grave looked grimly real to me.

Why We Become Sick

Admitting the presence of illness as we honestly ought to do, and confessing the reality of death as any sane person should, we, therefore, who are followers of the dear Lord, have a responsibility to search the mind and will of God to ask for a reason. Why are we sick? What are the causes of illness? The Holy Scriptures are ready to answer fully and explicitly. The Bible reveals that some sickness is of Satanic origin. In some way that we cannot understand, God permits it. When the Saviour healed the woman who had an infirmity eighteen years, "and was bowed together and could in no wise lift herself," He said in defense of His healing her on the Sabbath Day, "And ought not this woman, being a daughter of Abraham, whom Satan hath bound, lo, these eighteen years, be loosed from this bond on the sabbath day?" Her grievous affliction was the work of Satan (Luke 13:11-16). In Peter's sermon to the household of Cornelius at Caesarea he recounted, "How God anointed Jesus of Nazareth with the Holy Ghost and with power: who went about doing good, and healing all that were oppressed of the devil" (Acts 10:38). It is undeniable that sickness in large measure is a part of the evil work of Satan. One time, at least, God has given us an inward glimpse of the divine permission for that oppression. It is seen in the story of the old patriarch, Job. He was tried and he was afflicted that it might be proved he served God for love and not for personal gain.

Sometimes we are ill because of the chastening of the Lord. God not only permits but sometimes directs bodily affliction. If there is divine healing, there is also divine sickness. This is plainly seen in the life of

97

God's people, Israel (Exod. 15:26; Num. 11:33; Deut. 28:20-22, 27, 35, 60, 61; 2 Cor. 7:13). God's judgment through disease is seen in the leprosy of Miriam (Num. 12:9, 10), in the illness of David (Ps. 38:3-8), in the leprous curse upon Gehazi and his family (2 Kings 5:27), and in the smiting of Herod Agrippa I by the angel of the Lord (Acts 12:23). It is most interesting to read Josephus' account of the reason for the death of Herod Agrippa and compare it with the record in Acts (Ant. 19, 8, 2). Undeniably, some sicknesses are judgments from the hand of the Lord. Paul's solemn admonitions concerning the reverence by which we should partake of the Lord's Supper are fortified by the heavy reminder that because of the Corinthians' irreverence "many are weak and sickly among you, and many sleep." Some have even died under this judgment of God. The Apostle continued: "For if we would judge ourselves, we should not be judged . . . we are chastened of the Lord" (1 Cor. 11:30-32). This chastening of God is minutely discussed by the author of the Hebrews in his famous passage 12:5-13. If we are true sons and not illegitimates, then we can expect to be corrected from the hand of the Lord. Our illnesses may be because of heaven's discipline of us that we become better children of the Great King.

Without doubt, sometimes we are sick for the glory of God. Job was. Most emphatically Jesus said the man born blind was. Let us read again John 9:1-3: "And as Jesus passed by, he saw a man which was blind from his birth. And his disciples asked him, saying, Master, who did sin, this man, or his parents, that he was born blind? Jesus answered, Neither hath this man sinned, nor his parents: but that the works of God should be made manifest in him." Jesus said a like word regarding the terminal illness of Lazarus of Bethany, "This sickness is not unto death, but for the glory of God, that the Son of God might be glorified thereby" (John 11:4).

Violating God's Laws of Health

Many times, yes, so very many times, are we sick because we have violated God's laws of health. We do not eat right, we do not drink right, we do not breathe right, we do not sleep right, we do not exercise right; then we wonder why we are sick. We do not eat right. The medical profession looked through the records of over a million deaths in the United States and discovered that seventy percent of these deaths were caused by diseases associated with overweight. We dig our graves with our teeth. We do not drink right. The human system was not built for the consumption of alcohol. It is a damaging drug when drunk as a beverage. The alarming increase in alcoholism in the United States harbingers the dissolution of the very fabric of our national strength. This week I clipped out of our daily newspaper a report from a nationally famous doctor. I quote from the article: "A recent survey shows some eighty-five percent of our present teenagers drink. What starts teenagers on alcohol? There are two causes: One is their desire to belong, to be one of the group. The second cause is the most serious — it is home environment where parents drink. Abstaining families have the greatest number of abstaining children. The seriousness of adolescent drinking is shown in one statistic: that we are producing five hundred thousand new alcoholics every year, a new crop under way every twelve months. We are producing far more alcoholics than college graduates."

We do not breathe right. The respiratory system was not made to inhale through incessant days the smoke of burning material. Because of our breathing-smoking habits, over fifty thousand Americans die every year of lung cancer alone. Reader's Digest entitled an article on cigarette use "Cancer by the Carton." Sometimes I hear cigarettes referred to as "coffin nails" and "cancer sticks." Heart attacks are twenty-five percent more frequent among smokers. Because money is involved in both alcohol and tobacco, it is well nigh impossible to control their use, but death rides in the profit nonetheless. We do not jump off a building without paying the consequences of violating God's ordinances. What is true of the laws of gravity is also true of the laws of health. God is the author of them both.

We do not rest right, relax right, sleep right. We are tormented with anxieties, distractions and fears. We worry ourselves into sickness through lack of confidence in God. We cross a thousand bridges before we reach them; live under the pressure of a thousand possible confrontations that never materialize. We try to live, not one day at a time, but a dozen days or a whole year at a time. In the Sermon on the Mount, five times in the passage on trusting God does Jesus use the word *merimnao*. What does the word mean? Its use is clearly demonstrated in Paul's injunction to the Christians at Philippi when he said, "Be careful for nothing [*merimnao*]; but in every thing by prayer and supplication with thanksgiving let your requests be made known unto God" (Phil. 4:6). The Greek word *merimnao* refers to fretful distraction, worrisome anxiety, cankering care. Jesus says we are not to be like that, worried by fears of any tomorrow. We are to rest in the goodness and in the love of God (Matt. 6: 25-34). In all of these ways by which God can bless us and bestow health upon us, Daniel is an abounding illustration. He was taken captive by the Babylonians in 605 B.C. He lived through the seventy years of the captivity. He was thrown into the den of lions when an old man. He was still sound in body three years after Israel had returned to their land under the decree of Cyrus (Dan. 10:1). His temperate life was surpassed only by his trust in God (Dan. 1:8, 14-16). This is the way of strength and health.

Why are we sick? Sometimes we fall ill because of the burdens of service. Even Daniel fell into sickness because of the revelations given him (Dan. 8:26, 27). The godly friend of Paul and servant of the church at Philippi, Epaphroditus, came nigh unto death because of his disregard for health in his dedication to the word of the Lord (Phil. 2:25-30). We need to rest. This injunction was enforced upon the children of Israel when they sought to gather manna on the Sabbath day. The story in Exodus 16:27-30 reads:

> And it came to pass, that there went out some of the people on the seventh day for to gather, and they found none. And the LORD said unto Moses, How long refuse ye to keep my commandments and my laws? See, for that the LORD hath given you the sabbath, therefore he giveth you on the sixth day the bread of two days; abide ye every man in his place, let no man go out of his place on the seventh day. So the people rested on the seventh day.

There was no manna on the seventh day. One day in seven is to be a day of cessation from all labor. Even Jesus said to His disciples when they were so busy preaching, healing, and casting out demons that they had "no leisure so much as to eat," "Come ye yourselves apart into a desert place, and rest a while" (Mark 6:31). No man can ever do all the work. The discipline of self-limitation is difficult to achieve but it must be exercised by every servant of God.

Why are we sick? Sometimes it is for our spiritual deepening. Paul thus looked upon his "infirmities," his sicknesses (2 Cor. 12:7-10). The psalmist humbly writes in Psalm 119:67, "Before I was afflicted I went astray." Then he writes in Psalm 119:71, "It is good for me that I have been afflicted." Pain, sorrow, and sickness usually have one of two effects upon those who are forced to face the dark night in the deep valley; they either embitter the sufferer or they draw him closer to God.

What the Christian Should Do in Illness

What should the Christian do in illness? How are we to meet sickness? We are to meet the heavy day of our infirmity with faith in God. We are to take it to God in prayer. The Apostle John wrote to his friend, the well-beloved Gaius, that he prayed for him that he be in health (3 John 2). James, the pastor of the church at Jerusalem, wrote, "The prayer of faith shall save the sick" (James 5:15). When King Hezekiah was told by the prophet Isaiah that his sickness was unto death, Hezekiah took it to the Lord in prayer. So much of healing is bound up with faith. Turn to Matthew, chapter nine, and look at the marvelous healings in that narrative. Faith is offered unto God by four different people and groups of people in that one chapter alone. Matthew 9:1-8 recounts the healing of the palsied man through the faith of the four men who carried him (even through the roof) to Jesus. "Jesus seeing *their* faith said. . . ." Matthew 9:22 records the faith of the one who is healed, "Thy faith hath made thee whole." Matthew 9:25 describes the faith of the Healer, Himself. Matthew 9:27-30 recounts the faith of both the Healer and the ones who were healed. "And Jesus saith unto them, Believe ye that I am able to do this? They said unto him, Yea, Lord. Then touched he their eyes, saying, According to your faith be it unto you." The faith of the recipient is vital (Mark 10:52; Acts 14:9). The faith of the healer is no less needed (Matt. 17:19, 20; Acts 3:1-7).

Unbelief utterly destroys hope in the healing of a sufferer (Matt. 13:58). Encouragement to faith is seen in the methods Jesus used to heal. Twice Jesus made clay of spittle to anoint the eyes of the blind (John 9:6; Mark 8:23). Once He did it for the deaf (Mark 7:32). Spittle was believed to be efficacious in the healing art. Jesus used it as a visible means to help the man in himself. Somehow it is easier to believe when visible means are used. Human beings living in this natural world seem to grope for visible signs to stimulate their faith. Thus did Gideon with his fleece of wool in Judges 6:36-40. Thus did Hezekiah with his request for the shadow to return on the sundial of Ahaz in 2 Kings 20:8-11. Thus anointing oil was used in Mark 6:13 and James 5:14, 15. Medical science would be the first to recognize the dependence of the physical upon the spiritual. There is control of bodily functions by the subconscious self. One's mental, spiritual, emotional attitude has much to do with one's healing. A mighty faith in God is in itself mighty adjunct to triumphant therapeutics. Phychosomatic diseases are those illnesses caused by aberrations of the mind. To be well in the inner man contributes to our being well in the outward man. The two so often go together.

How shall the Christian meet illness? He shall meet it with God's means for healing. Look at Isaiah 38:21. Even though God had said to the praying king, "I have heard thy prayer, I have seen thy tears: behold I will add unto thy days fifteen years," yet the prophet said, "Let them take a lump of figs, and lay it for a plaister upon the boil, and he shall recover." God healed Hezekiah according to His miraculous word, but God did not disdain to use means in doing it. Jesus referred to the gracious ministries of the physicians: "But when Jesus heard that, he said unto them, They that be whole need not a physician, but they that are sick" (Matt. 9:12). In recounting the story of the Good Samaritan, the Lord said the kindness of the Samaritan prompted him to pour into the wounds of the beaten pilgrim "oil and wine" (Luke 10:34). The resurrected, glorified Saviour counseled the worldly church at Laodicea to "anoint thine eyes with eye-salve, that thou mayest see" (Rev. 3:18). Both the Apostle Paul and the beloved physician, Dr. Luke, healed the sick on the island of Melita (Malta). Paul laid hands on the sick and *iaomai*, "healed them." Luke practiced medi-

103

cine on other of those who had diseases and *therapeuo*, "healed them." So reads Acts 28:8, 9. For verse ten continues, "Who also honoured us [plural] with many honours; and when we [plural] departed, they laded us [plural] with such things as were necessary." The preacher and the doctor are here working together, the preacher praying to God and *iaomai*, "healing"; the doctor practicing medicine and *therapeuo*, "healing." The two different Greek verbs used and the plural pronouns used have tremendous significance. Modern movements of hostility to medicine are mistakes and unscriptural. To disregard means of healing is like a farmer who prays for a harvest but who sits down to see God do it alone. God has given to us means of healing as well as the desire to be healed. Medicines come from Him. Without His creative work they would not be in existence in this earth. Penicillin has been here from the dawn of time. It is just now that we have discovered it (not invented it). God made it. If you are sick in eye, or tooth, or ear, or body, trust in the Lord and call for "the beloved physician," a Dr. Luke to prescribe and a Preacher Paul to pray. That is the way to get well.

Glorifying God in Our Illnesses

How shall the Christian meet sickness? With committal to the sovereign purposes of God. The Lord can heal. The Lord has healed. The Lord does heal. The Lord may not heal. The Lord may take His servant home. Surely, surely, there is no more pitiful, pathetic appeal in all literature than the prayer of Moses to God that the Lord let him live to go over "this Jordan." The story reads:

> And I besought the LORD at that time, saying, O LORD GOD, thou hast begun to shew thy servant thy greatness, and thy mighty hand: for what God is there in heaven or in earth, that can do according to thy works, and according to thy might? I pray thee,

let me go over, and see the good land that is beyond Jordan, that goodly mountain, and Lebanon. But the LORD was wroth with me for your sakes, and would not hear me: and the LORD said unto me, Let it suffice thee; speak no more unto me of this matter, Get thee up into the top of Pisgah, and lift up thine eyes westward, and northward, and southward, and eastward, and behold it with thine eyes: for thou shalt not go over this Jordan (Deut. 3:23-27).

I turn the pages to Deuteronomy 34:4-6. There, before the Lord, Moses died on the east side of the Jordan. We all shall die in the will of God. It is just a question of when and how. None of us can escape. We shall grow old (if we outlive our youth) and die. The sentence of death has never been cancelled. The *last* enemy that is to be destroyed is death (1 Cor. 15:26; Rev. 20:14). To pray exception from this sentence is not faith but presumption. In God's sovereign purpose we shall die, but we shall not die until He wills our decease. When we die, it will be *His* gracious hands that open the door into the upper and better world. He has the keys of life and of death.

When that day comes, the hour of our heavenly translation and coronation, we are to glorify God in our yielded surrender. Jesus prayed in dark Gethsemane, "O my Father, if this cup may not pass away from me, except I drink it, thy will be done" (Matt. 26:42). He suffered and died upon the cruel tree in the sovereign purpose of God. Out of His death came life; out of His sufferings, salvation; out of His weakness, strength. He glorified God and redeemed us in His agony and death. The risen Saviour in turn said to His chief apostle, Simon Peter, "Verily, verily, I say unto thee, When thou was young, thou girdest thyself, and walkedst whither thou wouldst: but when thou shalt be old, thou shalt stretch forth thy hands, and another shall gird thee, and carry thee whither thou would not. This spake he, signifying by what death he should glorify God. And, when he had spoken this, he said unto him, Follow me" (John 21:18,19). Simon Peter is to die by outstretched hands; that is, by crucifixion.

This is the most cruel, agonizing form of execution ever devised by the depraved mind of man. But what is God's choice for Peter? Is it that he suffer and die in the most horrible way possible? Yes. But there is more. "This spake [Jesus], signifying by what death he should glorify God." We glorify God not in our songs sung when all goes well, when we are healthy and happy and affluent, when everything is going our way. An infidel can sing then. We glorify God in our songs sung in the night, when the dark day comes, when evil assails us, when we are afflicted, tormented, cast down to the ground. To praise God thus is to be triumphant in the faith, to win the crown of glory. This is the Christian way to meet sickness and death.

Chapter 13

The Gift of Speaking in Tongues

1 Corinthians 14

6 Now, brethren, if I come unto you speaking with tongues, what shall I profit you, except I shall speak to you either by revelation, or by knowledge, or by prophesying, or by doctrine?

7 And even things without life giving sound, whether pipe or harp, except they give a distinction in the sounds, how shall it be known what is piped or harped?

8 For if the trumpet give an uncertain sound, who shall prepare himself to the battle?

9 So likewise ye, except ye utter by the tongue words easy to be understood, how shall it be known what is spoken? for ye shall speak into the air.

At one time there was a weekly, nation-wide television program featuring a crime buster. The series was immensely popular. In every story a situation was developed in which the star detective would say to a witness he was questioning: "Just the facts, Mister. Just state the facts." This is preeminently what is needed in a Scriptural discussion of the gift of speaking in tongues. "Just give us the facts, preacher. Just tell us the facts." With God's help, we shall do just this.

In three places in the Book of Acts, speaking in tongues is mentioned; namely, at Pentecost (Acts 2: 1-11), in Caesarea (Acts 10:44-46), and in Ephesus (Acts 19:1-6). In Jerusalem, on the day of Pentecost, the outpouring of the Holy Spirit was attended by three miracles: one, the sound of a rushing, mighty wind; two, the sight of a great flame of fire that, descending, divided into tongues which burned above the heads of the apostolic witnesses; three, the hearing on the part of men from the nations of the civilized world, each in his own tongue, the wondrous words of God. The gift of tongues at Pentecost was one in which the language spoken was understood by the different nationals. No interpreter was necessary. The languages spoken were *not* unknown tongues. They were the native languages of the hearing people.

This unusual phenomenon was repeated at Caesarea in the household of the Roman centurion, Cornelius. Simon Peter described the outpouring as "the like gift" as the apostles had experienced at Pentecost (Acts 11:17). Could it have been that in the household of the centurion there were soldiers, slaves, servants, and governmental officials from many of the nations of the Roman world? Could it have been that in their superlative, heavenly ecstasy they reverted each to his mother tongue in praising God for so great a salvation? It is a most commonplace psychological truth that in moments of extreme peril or delight a foreigner will exclaim in his native language "in which he was born," rather than in the later language he has more recently acquired.

Similar expressions of ecstasy were poured out before the Lord in the case of the twelve disciples of John the Baptist at Ephesus. When Paul met these twelve men, he immediately sensed that something was tragically wrong with their faith. He asked, therefore, the simple question, "Did you receive the Holy Spirit *when* you believed" (Greek, *pisteusantes*, not "since ye believed" as the King James version, but "*when* ye believed.") These men replied that they had never heard of the Holy Spirit. Now, John the Baptist preached the Holy Spirit (cf. Matt. 3:11). Why do these followers of John, then avow that they never heard of the Third Person of the Deity? For the simple reason that the true message of John had been lost as it was passed down from disciple to disciple to disciple. The John the Baptist movement continued alongside the Christian movement for many, many years. When these misled men, who were converts of of the converts of the converts of John the Baptist, heard the saving message of the Son of God they received the mercy of the Lord Jesus, they were baptized; and when Paul in prayer and consecration laid his hands upon their heads, they broke forth in marvelous praises to God. As at Caesarea, did each speak in his own native tongue? Ephesus was a polyglot city and each man could have come from a different part of the Roman world. In their celestial joy the dozen men spoke in languages (plural) and prophesied (exhorted in the faith unto edification, spoke by holy inspiration).

The Unknown Tongues of Corinth

Aside from these three instances in the Book of Acts, one other place in the New Testament mentions the phenomenon of speaking in tongues. It is in Paul's long discussion of the gifts of the Spirit in 1 Corinthians 12:1-14. In 1 Corinthians 12:10 Paul names one of the charismata as being "divers kinds of tongues." In 1 Corinthians 14:1-40 the Apostle discusses this gift. Apparently, the speaking in tongues that characterized the assembly of the Corinthian Church was totally unlike the miraculous gift at Pentecost. At Pentecost the disciples spoke in known, understood languages. No interpreter was needed. At Corinth the language was unknown. Paul writes in 1 Corinthians 14:2: "He that speaketh in an unknown tongue speaketh not unto men, but unto God; for no man understandeth him." Again, Paul says in 1 Corinthians 14:14: "For if I pray in an unknown tongue, my spirit prayeth, but my understanding is unfruitful." For this reason the speaker in an unknown tongue had to have by his side one who

109

had the gift of interpretation (1 Cor. 14:27, 28), or else he had to be given the gift of interpretation himself (1 Cor. 14:5, 13).

This outbreak of speaking in unknown tongues at Corinth is an amazing development. It is utterly unlike anything we have ever witnessed before in the kingdom of God. The phenomenon is not in the Old Testament. At times and in places the saints of the Old Testament were filled with the Holy Spirit as well as the saints of the New Testament, but never in their lives is seen anything like this. All the other gifts of the Spirit are seen in their lives, but not this. The phenomenon is not seen in the life and experience of our Lord Jesus. He was filled with the Holy Spirit (Luke 3:21, 22; 4:1, 14, 18, etc.). All the other gifts of the Spirit can be found in Him beautifully, gloriously. But not this. Nor can I imagine, in my wildest imagination, the blessed Saviour speaking in unknown tongues. It does not fit. It does not become Him. He never did it. Never. Nor is such a phenomenon mentioned in any of the gospels. The most spiritual book of the New Testament, the gospel of John, never refers to it, nor even approaches such a thing.

The gift of speaking in tongues is not found in the charismatic lists in Romans 12:6-8; Ephesians 4:11. With the exception of this passage in 1 Corinthians, the gift is never referred to in any of the epistles of Paul. It is not mentioned in the pastoral letters (1, 2 Timothy, Titus), it is not mentioned in the Book of Hebrews, it is not mentioned in the General Epistles (James, 1, 2 Peter, 1, 2, 3 John, Jude), and it is never mentioned in the Revelation. With the exception of Corinth, the phenomenon is never seen in any of the churches of the New Testament; it is not in the churches of Macedonia, Achaia, Judaea, Samaria, Asia, Rome, or any other place. It is seen only in the church at Corinth, a congregation that Paul called "carnal" (1 Cor. 3:1-3), and a people whom Paul described as

110

"babes in Christ" (1 Cor. 3:1). The gift of tongues was not nearly so prominent in the early churches as those who advocate it would have us believe. At the most, it was a rare phenomenon found only in a few places, and, as far as we know, in only one church, and that not a spiritual church but a carnal one filled with every problem and disorder.

A Problem to the Apostle Paul

"Just the facts, preacher. Just give us the facts." Let us look at 1 Corinthians 14:1-40 and write down the plain facts. As we read the discussion, one fact stands out above all others. It is this: speaking in tongues is plainly a problem. The church is having serious trouble with it and Paul is wrestling with it (cf. 1 Cor. 14:23, 39). If the church at Corinth had been giving itself to prayer, to praise, to love, to soul-winning, to intercession, to sacrifice, to giving, or to any one of a thousand other Christian virtues, the Apostle would have written them words of deepest, sincerest commendation. But *this!* This is a problem and a heavy one. The discussion of Paul is not a list of exhortations to speak in tongues, but a long enumeration of restrictions against the practice. The Apostle is not encouraging the Corinthians to exercise the gift but to refrain from its use. He is not presenting a set of rules to glorify the congregation in tongue-speaking, but he is rather laying down stringent regulations to restrain this thing that has broken out in the church. Paul is hedging the gift on every side.

Let us cite here every sympathetic word of toleration that Paul writes concerning the exercise of tongue-speaking and see if he does not qualify the use with an appeal for something else. In 1 Corinthians 14:4 the Apostle writes, "He that speaketh in an unknown tongue edifieth himself." Then, he writes the better alternative, "But he that prophesieth edifieth the church." In 1 Corinthians 14:5 he writes, "I would that ye all spake with tongues." Then he qualifies the sentence with this addendum: "But rather that ye prophesied: for greater is he that prophesieth than he that speaketh with tongues." In 1 Corinthians 14: 18 the Apostle says, "I thank my God, I speak with tongues more than ye all." (There is no record that he ever used the gift. Could he be referring to his messages to the different nations to which God sent him as an apostle to the Gentiles?) Then, he qualifies this startling statement with the most stringent avowal of all: "Yet in the church I had rather speak five words with my understanding, that by my voice I might teach others also, than ten thousand words in an unknown tongue." There is one other passage of toleration in this Corinthian discussion. It is 1 Corinthians 14:39, where the Apostle says: "Forbid not to speak with tongues." But in the same sentence he again qualifies the permission with an earnest alternative, "Wherefore, brethren, covet to prophesy [not to speak in tongues]."

Having written down every word of toleration on the part of the Apostle Paul concerning speaking in unknown tongues, now we shall look at some of the vigorous statements he uses against the practice. The first is 1 Corinthians 14:19: "Yet in the church I had rather speak five words with my understanding, that by my voice I might teach others also, than ten thousand words in an unknown tongue." These are tremendous odds — five to ten thousand! This would be enough to allay the practice forever in the judgment of any ordinary, fair-minded person. The practice has no place in the church.

Another heavy, uncompromising mandate of the Apostle is 1 Corinthians 14:34, 35. Under no conditions is a woman to speak in an unknown tongue in the church. In this passage on tongue-speaking, Paul says: "Let your women keep silence in the churches: for it is not permitted unto them to speak; but they are commanded to be under obedience, as also saith the law. And if they will learn any thing, let them ask their husbands at home: for it is a shame for women to speak in the church." What does the Apostle mean, "It is a shame for women to speak in the church"? In 1 Corinthians 11:3-10 he had just given instructions how the women were to dress when they prayed or when they prophesied in the church. Now, here in 1 Corinthians 14:34, 35, he excludes their speaking in no uncertain terms. Has he lost his mind? Is he stupid? Has he already forgotten what he has just written? No, not at all. What the Apostle is saying is most plain and most pertinent. These verses on women not speaking in the church are imbedded in the middle of this chapter on speaking in tongues. He is not interdicting women's praying or prophesying in public worship (he had already given directions permitting that in 1 Cor. 11:3-10); he is interdicting their speaking in *tongues* in public worship. The woman is not to do it. But why is the Apostle so severe about women exercising the gift of tongue-speaking. Here again the answer is plain.

In front of the ancient city of Corinth was the deep blue sea. Behind the city of Corinth was the steep, high Acro-Corinthus, an Acropolis far more prominent than that in Athens on which was built the Parthenon. Crowning the imposing Acropolis at Corinth was a magnificent temple to Aphrodite (Latin, "Venus"). The Greek goddess of love and beauty was worshiped with sexual orgies. The temple prostitutes who were used in these orgies of worship worked themselves up into ecstatic frenzies as they followed their heathen, immoral rituals. The sight of frenzied women speaking in unknown tongues in their dedication to immorality was a common one in the days of Graeco-Roman culture. Paul's abhorrence of such speaking is explicable and obvious. Paul assumes that even strangers walking by an assembly of God's people, seeing and

113

hearing the women talking in unknown tongues, would immediately say: "What have we here; a little colony of Aphrodite? Let us go in and enjoy the sensual pleasure." "No," said the Apostle, "a thousand times no! When it comes to speaking in tongues, let your women keep silence in the churches. It is a shame [mark this word 'shame'] for women to speak in unknown tongues in the church." That interdiction still stands, unremoved. The hysterical, unseemly excess of tongue-speaking women in public worship is a reproach to the name of the Lord.

A Sign to the Jewish Nation

In 1 Corinthians 14:21, 22 Paul discusses the purpose of the gift of speaking in tongues. He says that it is a sign to the unbelieving Jewish nation. From the Old Testament (from 'the law" as Paul here calls the entire Hebrew Scriptures) he quotes Isaiah 28:11, 12 regarding the refusal of Israel to hearken to Jehovah when He spoke to them in plain, understandable language. "Therefore," said the Lord God to the people of Israel, "since you will not hear me when I speak to you in clearness and simplicity in your own tongue, I shall now speak to you in languages which you cannot understand." (In the historical situation in which Isaiah is delivering the prophecy, God says He will speak in the foreign, strange languages of the Assyrians and the Babylonians, who were used by the Lord to chasten His disobedient people, Israel.) Paul takes this passage from Isaiah to show that speaking in tongues was a sign to the lost, Christ-rejected nation of Israel. This can be easily seen in the signs at Pentecost given to the men of Jerusalem and Judaea (Acts 2:14). Of the three miraculous attestations of God to the reality of the heavenly outpouring of the Holy Spirit, one was the gift of speaking in "other" tongues. We see this attestation of heaven's will in the marvelous miracle

114

of tongues that confirmed the inclusion of the Gentiles into the body of Christ at Caesarea. The proof to the Jewish brethren at Jerusalem that the Gentiles were to be also a part of the salvation of our Lord was seen in the sign of tongues. So writes Luke in Acts 10: 44-48. So said Simon Peter in his report to the Jewish church at Jerusalem in Acts 11:15-17. The marvelous gift of speaking in these languages was a sign to the disbelieving nation of Israel.

But to the heathen, pagan, unbelieving Gentiles the phenomenon is anything but a sign. To the Gentile world it was plain idiocy. Paul continues in 1 Corinthians 14:23-25: "If therefore the whole church be come together into one place, and all speak with tongues, and there come in those that are unlearned, or unbelievers, will they not say that ye are mad? But if all prophesy, and there come in one that believeth not, or one unlearned, he is convinced of all, he is judged of all: And thus are the secrets of his heart made manifest; and so falling down on his face he will worship God, and report that God is in you of a truth." Look at this passage carefully. The Apostle avows that if a pagan unbeliever walking down the streets of Corinth passed by an assembly of the Church and, stopping by, saw and heard them speaking in tongues, that pagan would certainly say, "Ye are mad." The Greek word translated "mad" is mainomai, which means, "to be insane," "to rave as a madman." Is not this obvious? Could you imagine Paul on Mars' Hill, speaking before the Areopagus (the Supreme Court of the Athenians) in an unknown tongue, and Silas by his side doing the interpreting? Would they not have said that those two Jews were insane? The same effect is produced upon the pagan world today by those who would do such a thing. According to Paul, in 1 Corinthians 14:23, the effect produced upon the unbeliever is that we who name the name of Christ are raving madmen.

The Demand for a Sign

There were four sign gifts bestowed upon the witness of Christ during the transitional days of the Apostolic Age, while the New Testament Scriptures were being written. One of these sign gifts was speaking in tongues. When the authenticating necessity for the sign gift ceased, the phenomenon ceased. It was needed no longer. It had served its purpose. For us to seek to re-create the sign is not faith but presumption. In the days of Moses, God authenticated the law-giver with signs and miracles. With his rod, for example, he parted the Red Sea. What would you think of a people who said to Jehovah: "God, you did it one time; now let's see you do it again"? Elijah was taken up into heaven in a whirlwind. What would you think about a people who would demand of every prophet a like sign, that he be taken up into glory in a chariot of fire? "You did it one time, Lord; now do it again!" When Jesus was born, the angelic hosts praised God and a star led the Magi to the manger in Bethlehem. What would you think of a people who demanded that the signs be repeated for us to see? "Let us see that star and let us hear those angels praise God." At Pentecost and at Caesarea, and in a few other places, a sign was given to attest the marvelous outpouring of the Spirit. What about the demand that the authenticating sign be repeated and repeated and repeated? "Do it again, Lord. Do it again." The need for the sign ceased (and that most early) and the phenomenon ceased. It is now useless, just as useless as if someone went down to the Red Sea and divided it again with a miraculous rod. As Paul emphatically concluded in 1 Corinthians 13:8, "Tongues shall cease."

We have the complete Bible. We have the open Book before us, God's Holy Scriptures. The need now is for plain language, understandable language, simple language. Paul so exhorted in 1 Corinthians 14:6-12. Listen to the Apostle as he makes the most sensible

116

appeal a man ever made: "Now, brethren, if I come unto you speaking with tongues, what shall I profit you, except I shall speak to you either by revelation, or by knowledge, or by prophesying, or by doctrine? And even things without life giving sound, whether pipe or harp, except they give distinction in the sounds, how shall it be known what is piped or harped? For if the trumpet give an uncertain sound, who shall prepare himself to the battle? So likewise ye, except ye utter by the tongue words easy to be understood, how shall it be known what is spoken? for ye shall speak into the air. There are, it may be, so many kinds of voices in the world, and none of them is without significance. Therefore if I know not the meaning of the voice, I shall be unto him that speaketh a barbarian, and he that speaketh shall be a barbarian unto me. Even so ye, forasmuch as ye are zealous of spiritual gifts, seek that ye may excell to the edifying of the church" (1 Cor. 14:6-12). This "sounding of the trumpet" reminds me of God's watchman in Ezekiel 33:1-11.

If you are an unbeliever, God calls you to faith, but not by signs, wonders or miracles. He will not use the parting of the Red Sea or the fire on Elijah's altar to speak to you. He will not use strange sounds or unearthly voices to speak to you. He will speak clearly, intelligently, understandably, by the Word. He will appeal to you in the Spirit of Isaiah 1:18: "Come now, and let us reason together, said the LORD: though your sins be as scarlet, they shall be as white as snow; though they be red like crimson, they shall be as wool." He will call you minus tongues, minus signs, minus miracles. He will call you by your simply trusting Jesus.

117

Chapter 14

The Interpretation of Tongues

1 Corinthians 14

13 Wherefore let him that speaketh in an unknown tongue pray that he may interpret.

27 If any man speak in an unknown tongue, let it be by two, or at the most by three, and that by course; and let one interpret.

28 But if there be no interpreter, let him keep silence in the church; and let him speak to himself, and to God.

Of the four charismatic sign gifts introducing the new Christian era, listed by Paul in 1 Corinthians 12:9 and 10 (the gift of healing, the gift of miracles, the gift of divers kinds of tongues), one is the gift of the interpretation of tongues. What is this "interpretation of tongues"?

If the "tongue" be a true foreign language, then to interpret it by one who knew the language would be no charisma, no grace-gift. Anyone, even an infidel familiar with the language, could do it. If the "tongue" be a true foreign language not understood by the speaker, and the interpreter does not understand it either, then we are witnessing a double miracle: to speak it and to interpret it. This is certainly a round about way to edify the Church, by means of a double-action miracle, a miracle of foreign speech followed by a miracle of interpretation. If the "tongue" be a series of ejaculations, broken and disjoined syllables, abrupt and exclamatory utterances (and the phenomenon in Corinth was this, 1 Cor. 14:2, 4, 14) then the gift of interpretation consisted of turning what seemed to be meaningless utterances into words easy to be under-

118

stood (1 Cor. 14:9). The interpretation could be made by the speaker himself if he had the gift (1 Cor. 14:5, 13), or, if he lacked the gift, by one who possessed it (1 Cor. 14:27, 28).

Trouble With Different Interpreters

Three things about the gift of interpretation are most noticeable in this discussion of Paul in 1 Corinthians 14:1-40. The first is this: Those who possessed the gift were well-known in the Church. No exercise of tongues was to be permitted in public if no interpreter was present (1 Cor. 14:28). The second obvious observation is this: One interpreter was looked upon as being capable and competent to interpret any tongue (1 Cor. 14:27). Whatever the number of tongue-speakers allowed to speak (Paul permitted three at the most), the interpretation was to be made by only one person. This leads to a third serious but painful conclusion: It is all too apparent that interpreters did not agree. When Paul appeals in all this outbreak that "all things be done decently and in order" (1 Cor. 14:40), and that "all things be done unto edifying" (1 Cor. 14:26), he names the sources of turmoil and dissension. He says the trouble is caused by the brethren who stand up in church with differing doctrines, revelations, tongues and interpretations (1 Cor. 14:26). It does not take much imagination to see what was happening in this disorderly church. When more than one interpreter was allowed to exercise his gift, those other interpreters did not always agree and trouble ensued. Therefore, the limitation Paul makes to one interpreter lest the church fall into a wrangle.

It would be most easy to choose sides in an altercation over whose interpretation of an unknown tongue was correct. Not understanding anything that was being said, anything could pass for the truth. But who would know? For no man understandeth him," as Paul says in 1 Corinthians 14:2. A seminary graduate who had majored in Hebrew attended a tongues meeting in California. In the midst of the meeting he stood up and quoted by memory the first Psalm in the original language. After he had finished, the interpreter arose and solemnly, piously made known in plain English what the brother had spoken in an unknown tongue. The interpreter made it an utterance, Spirit-inspired, about women prophesying in church. When the seminarian made known what he had done and what he had said, pandemonium broke loose. In such a Corinthian situation there is no limit to the possibilities of trouble. One sister might receive an utterance about the personal life of another saint in the sisterhood. There is no end to it, as Paul sorrowfully found in the troubled church at Corinth.

Paul's Interpretation of the Sign Gift

What is Paul's interpretation of tongues? In 1 Corinthians 14:19 he writes in no uncertain terms: "Yet in the church I had rather speak five words with my understanding, that by my voice I might teach others also, than ten thousand words in an unknown tongue." In 1 Corinthians 13:8-11 he writes of the cessation of the movement: "Charity never faileth: but whether there be prophecies, they shall fail; whether there be tongues, they shall cease; whether there be knowledge, it shall vanish away. For we know in part, and we prophesy in part. But when that which is perfect is come, then that which is in part shall be done away. When I was a child, I spake as a child, I thought as a child: but when I became a man, I put away childish things." Paul's use of verbs in 1 Corinthians 13:8 is most instructive and decisive. Of love, he says that it will never *ekpipto*, it will never "fall," "fail," (Greek, *pipto*, "to fall," *ek*, "from"). Of the gifts of prophecy, he says that they will be rendered useless (Greek, *katargethesontai*, future passive of *katargeo*, "to render useless," "to make inoperative"). After the writing of the New Testament Scriptures, the gift of the prophet to tell the Church what to do and what to believe will be no longer needed. Our appeal now is not to a man with the charismatic gift of prophecy but to the written Word of God. Of the gift of knowledge, Paul uses the same word, *katargethesontai*. The gift no longer will be needed to direct the Church in the knowledge of the Lord. We have the full, all-sufficient rule for faith and practice in the Holy Scriptures. Prophecies will "fail" (the word used in the King James translation), not in the sense that they will break down but rather in the sense that they will become unnecessary, useless. Knowledge will "vanish away" (the translation of the King James version), not in the sense that it has no contribution to make but in the sense of the fragment being swallowed up in the whole. When we have the complete Word (written now in the Bible, or personally present at His coming), we no longer need a small, incomplete, unfinished portion.

When Paul comes to speak of tongues in 1 Corinthians 13:8, he not only changes the verb but he also changes the voice of the verb he uses. As with "prophecies" and as with "knowledge" we would have expected him to use the future passive *katargethesontai*. Not so. He uses a different verb, *pauo*, "to cause to cease," and he changes the voice from passive to middle, *pausontai*, which literally translated means "tongues shall make themselves to cease," or "tongues shall automatically cease of themselves." Phillip's translation of the verse goes like this: "If there are prophecies they will be fulfilled and done with, if there are 'tongues' the need for them will disappear, if there be knowledge it will be swallowed up in truth."

Most emphatically Paul avows that "tongues will automatically cease of themselves." In the next verse, 1 Corinthians 13:9, they have already ceased in his thinking, for he mentions the gift of prophecy and he names the gift of knowledge but he pointedly omits

121

the gift of tongues. Tongues are needed no longer. This is not only seen as Paul writes in 1 Corinthians 13:9 but it is also vividly illustrated in his epistles written during the remaining years of his ministry. 1 Corinthians is one of Paul's earliest letters. It is preceded only by the two epistles to the church at Thessalonica. After Paul wrote 1 Corinthians, he wrote 2 Corinthians, but in this latter epistle he never refers to speaking in tongues. After Paul wrote 1 Corinthians, he wrote a letter to the churches of Galatia, but he never refers to tongues. After Paul wrote 1 Corinthians, he wrote the letter to the church at Rome, but he never refers to speaking in tongues. After Paul wrote 1 Corinthians, he wrote Philippians, and Colossians, and Philemon, and Ephesians, and the Pastoral Epistles of 1 Timothy and Titus and 2 Timothy, but in none of them does he ever mention speaking in tongues. Tongues is the first sign-gift that ceased. It ceased almost immediately. The sign belonged to the infancy of the Church. "When I was a child, I spake as a child, . . . but when I became a man, I put away childish things" (1 Cor. 13:11). The Church grew up and no longer needed the sign. To re-create the useless gift is to seek to return to the babyhood of the assemblies of Christ. To the grown man, the rattle and the teething ring have no purpose. They have been rendered useless.

Facts Concerning Modern Glossolalia

Since Paul wrote his interpretation of speaking in tongues, almost two thousand years have passed. In reviewing that long history and in observing the phenomenon of modern-day glossolalia, I have a definite interpretation that comes from the depth of my own soul. These observations will be made in factual presentations. "Just the facts, Mister. Just give us the facts." There are five of these plain, clearly recognized facts to be seen in ecclesiastical chronology and in contemporary Christendom.

First fact. The basic doctrine that lies back of glossolalian practice is wrong. That doctrine is this: that speaking in tongues is the necessary evidence of the filling [they use the word "baptism"] of the Holy Spirit. This doctrine is in direct opposition to the distinct and emphasized teaching of the Word of God. In 1 Corinthians 12:13 Paul says that all the Christians at Corinth had been baptized by the Holy Spirit, had been added to the body of Christ. But in 1 Corinthians 12:28-30 Paul avows that all do not speak with tongues. If you have been saved, you have been made a member by Spirit baptism of the precious body of our Lord. "By one Spirit are we all baptized into one body" (1 Cor. 12:13). But whether you speak with tongues or not has nothing to do with that holy, heavenly baptism. The two are in nowise connected; neither is one the evidence of the other.

Again in Ephesians 5:18 we are emphatically enjoined to be filled with the Spirit. It is God's will that all be filled with the Spirit. But here, also, it must be observed in contradistinction to this injunction that we all be filled with the Spirit. The Apostle writes that we are not all given the gift of tongues. "Are all apostles? [No.] Are all prophets? [No.] Are all workers of miracles? [No.] Have all the gifts of healing? [No.]" Do all speak with tongues? [No]" (1 Cor. 12:29, 30). There is no such Scriptural teaching as that speaking in tongues is the sign of the filling ("baptism") of the Holy Spirit. It is a man-made doctrine and does not come from the Bible.

Second fact. In the years of my reading through Christian history and of my studying the lives of great men of God, I have never once found an instance where a mighty hero of the faith spoke in unknown tongues. Preachers, missionaries, theologians, pioneers, translators, evangelists, all have come under review, but glossolalia is never a part of their lives. John Wesley will describe his Aldersgate experience, but never will he approach such a thing as speaking in

123

tongues. Charles G. Finney will write in his famous *Autobiography* the fillings of the Holy Spirit that came in waves over his soul, but never will he intimate that he spoke in tongues. Dwight L. Moody will describe his marvelous infilling of love that swept his very being, but never does he suggest that he spoke in tongues. R. A. Torrey will write in a book on the baptism of the Holy Spirit, but his words of experience are pointedly directed against glossolalia. There is no exception to this witness, whether the great man of God lived in the ancient or the medieval or the modern world. John Chrysostom (John the Golden-mouth,) possibly the most eloquent preacher of all time and one of the most gifted commentators on the Scriptures, born in A.D. 345, pastor of the churches at Antioch and Constantinople, expressed even in his day puzzlement at Paul's account of the tongue-speaking situation at Corinth. He said: "The whole passage (1 Cor. 14: 1-40) is exceedingly obscure and the obscurity is occasioned by our ignorance of the facts and the cessation of happinings which were common in those days but unexampled in our own." Glossolalia is always outside the circle of the life and experience of the great men of God who lived in Christian history.

Third fact. In the long story of the Church, after the days of the apostles, wherever the phenomenon of glossolalia has appeared it has been looked upon as heresy. Glossolalia mostly has been confined to the nineteenth and twentieth centuries. But wherever and however its appearance, it has never been accepted by the historical churches of Christendom. It has been universally repudiated by these churches as a doctrinal and emotional aberration.

The Amazing Way We Are Supposed to Receive the Baptism of the Holy Ghost

Fourth fact. Modern glossolalia is a bewildering development. In the last century (after a silence in tongue-speaking for hundreds of years) there appeared in England a man by the name of Edward Irving who presented himself as a prophet of God. He dressed like one (with long, uncut hair) and he looked like one (with a towering stature). He and his "Irvingites" began the tongue-speaking movement that has reached down to us today. Of him, rugged old Thomas Carlyle said, "God is evidently working miracles by hysterics."

The program of the glossolaliasts to teach us how to speak in tongues is something new for the books. A few days ago I received through the mail a tract concerning how to receive the "baptism" of the Holy Ghost and how to speak in unknown tongues. I quote from the tract: "How can I receive the Holy Ghost? All you have to do to be saved is to raise your hands up toward Heaven and turn your head up toward Heaven and begin praising God just as fast as you can and let your tongue go and let the Holy Ghost come in. Thousands of people receive the Holy Ghost this way. You can receive it too, if you will just let the Holy Ghost speak through your tongue." A book that I read, from a famous glossolaliast, gave specific instructions how anyone could receive the "baptism" of the Holy Ghost. "Raise up your hands and your eyes to heaven," he said, "and begin speaking words, sounds, syllables, and keep it up, faster, faster, faster, louder, louder words, more words, faster, faster, and it has happened! You have received the baptism of the Holy Ghost!" Seekers after the "baptism" are encouraged to remain in "tarrying meetings" in which they are taught to loosen the tongue by imitation of the leader in saying "ah-bah, ah-bah, beta, beta," etc. The leader will shake the lower jaw of a seeker to loosen it so that the gift will come. What am I to think about all of this? Is the Holy Third Person of the Trinity, the moving, mighty Spirit of God, thus controlled and directed by the loosening of the joints of the jaw? By the gibberish of senseless sounds? I am bewildered by the suggestion.

Fifth fact. As far as I have been able to learn, no real language is ever spoken by the glossolaliast. He truly speaks in an unknown and unknowable tongue. Tape recordings of those speaking in unknown tongues were played before the Toronto Institute of linguistics. After these learned men in the science of phonetics had studied the recordings, they said, "This is no human language." At another time, other tape recordings were played before a group of governmental linguists at our nation's capitol. These gifted men found the sounds unrecognizable. "What they speak is meaningless to the human ear," was their verdict.

Sixth fact. Whatever and whenever glossolalia appears it is always hurtful and divisive. There is no exception to this. It is but another instrument for the tragic torture of the body of Christ. I have seen some of our finest churches torn apart by the practice. I have seen some of our churches that were lighthouses for Christ in a pioneer and pagan land destroyed by the doctrine. In a revival situation that promised many souls for Jesus and a true outpouring of the Holy Spirit, the leader decimated it all by beginning to speak in tongues. He came to see me in Dallas. I said to him: "Had you driven these many miles to come and see me to say, 'I have been filled with the Holy Spirit, I have been led of the Lord to give to the work of the Kingdom ninety percent of all I make and to live on the remaining ten percent,' I would have said, 'Praise God, Hallelujah!' Had you driven all the way to Dallas to say to me, "I have been filled with the Holy Spirit, I have resolved to pray six hours every day,' I would have said, 'Glory to God for such a commitment!' Had you come these many miles to my study to say to me, 'I have the visitation from heaven in my soul; I will win at least one person to Jesus every day,' I would have said, 'Bless the name of God for so meaningful a dedication!' But when you come over these many miles to see me and you say, 'I have received the baptism of the Holy Ghost, I am speaking in tongues,' I

126

reply, 'Oh, oh, oh! What a tragedy! The work of the revival is ruined.'" And it was. No revival came. Only trouble, disorder, and confusion, as at Corinth.

I close with the avowal of the Apostle Paul: "Yet in the church I had rather speak five words with my understanding, that by my voice I might teach others also, than ten thousand words in an unknown tongue" (1 Cor. 14:19).

Chapter 15

The More Excellent Way
(Love and the Gifts of the Spirit)

1 Corinthians 12

³¹ But covet earnestly the best gifts: and yet shew I unto you a more excellent way.

1 Corinthians 13

¹ Though I speak with the tongues of men and of angels, and have not charity, I am become as sounding brass, or a tinkling cymbal.

² And though I have the gift of prophecy, and understand all mysteries, and all knowledge; and though I have all faith, so that I could remove mountains, and have not charity, I am nothing.

³ And though I bestow all my goods to feed the poor, and though I give my body to be burned, and have not charity, it profiteth me nothing.

¹³ And now abideth faith, hope, charity, these three, but the greatest of these is charity.

The location of the greatest "love chapter" in the Bible is most amazing. It is placed in the middle of Paul's long discussion on spiritual gifts. Herein is a special message in itself. A large part of the importance of the thirteenth chapter of 1 Corinthians lies in its contextual placement. It is not as though the author set out to write a hymn on love. That would have been worthy, but it has nothing to do with this passage. The chapter is an integral part of the Apostle's presentation of the meaning and use of the gifts of the Spirit. Chapter twelve is a discussion of the purpose of the gifts. Chapter fourteen is a discussion of the perversion of the gifts (particularly tongues). Chapter thirteen, the in-between chapter, is a discussion of the sublimest, highest uses of the gifts.

Chapter twelve of 1 Corinthians introduces the long dissertation on the *pneumataka* (literally, "the spirituals"), the *charismata* (literally, "the grace gifts"). Paul, in this chapter, describes the gifts and their relationship to the church as a whole. He begins in 12:1 by saying that we all should have clear knowledge concerning spiritual gifts. Paul faced the same problem in his day that we face in our day; namely, ignorance concerning spiritual gifts. I would suppose the subject is the least understood by Christian people of any of the significant doctrines of the Bible. There are two extremes: one is abuse, excess and fanaticism. The other is the opposite pendulum reaction of neglect and cold formalism. Satan, also, is most eager and delighted to counterfeit the true gifts of the Spirit, even as Jannes and Jambres (2 Tim. 3:8) counterfeited the miracles of Moses and Aaron; as the false prophet Zedekiah opposed God's true prophet Micah, and as Simon Magus sought to use for money the marvelous outpouring of the Spirit.

Chapter thirteen of 1 Corinthians continues the discussion of the *pneumataka* begun in chapter twelve. In this passage Paul presents that love which alone gives the ministry of the gifts any value. Love in the use of the gifts of the Spirit is the fulfillment of every heavenly purpose, the remedy for every excess, and the protection against every error. Without love the gifts fail of their purpose.

Chapter fourteen of 1 Corinthians continues the discussion of the *pneumataka* begun in chapter thirteen. In this portion of the long section, the Apostle seeks to regulate the ministry of the gifts as they are exercised in the open assembly of the church, especially giving attention to the abuse of tongues.

The three chapters (1 Cor. 12, 13, 14) are inseparably linked. Chapter thirteen is not an interlude, as though the Apostle had burst into a song on love. It is an interlink between chapters twelve and fourteen in this discussion on the gifts of the Spirit. Chapter thirteen is not a digression or a change of direction regarding the subject. It is rather an intensification of the theme followed in chapters twelve and fourteen. Chapter thirteen is not a dissertation on love as such. The subject of chapter thirteen concerns the true motive for the use of spiritual gifts. The last verse of chapter twelve makes a plea for the more excellent "way" of blessedness in the use of the gifts. Every gift is to be baptized in love. The first verse of chapter fourteen follows almost the same Greek wording as is found in the last verse of chapter twelve. The gifts are to be subservient to the motive of love. The chapter between twelve and fourteen, chapter thirteen, deals with the gifts in the hands of love, the gifts controlled by love, the gifts motivated by love. Without love the gifts are willful and wayward, inevitably and eventually ministering to selfish pride. Without gifts, love becomes cheaply sentimental and unoccupied. With both love and gifts, the Lord glorifies His Word through His servants.

Love the Motive for the Use of Spiritual Gifts

The great theme of 1 Corinthians 13 is that love must be the actuating principle back of any employment of spiritual gifts. It is love that renders the *charismata* blessed and profitable. Verse one avows that the gift of tongues, whether of men or of angels, however eloquent or fervent, will not profit or bless the speaker without love. "I [not the gift] am become as sounding brass [metal castanets] or a tinkling cymbal." Without compassionate sympathy for those listening, eloquence in speaking only accentuates the emptiness of the heart of the speaker. He sounds, and he is, hollow. There are those with no greatness but in forensic speech. There are those whose whole genius expires in a fray of words and in forms of easily forgotten rhetoric. Only love can give any real power to eloquence. The dead heart and the selfish soul need the live coals from off the altar of God's compassion to touch their lips. Otherwise, their speaking gift is empty vanity.

Verse two of 1 Corinthians 13 avows that the sublimest gifts of prophecy, knowledge, and faith are profitless to the possessor of the gifts without love. "I [not the gifts] am nothing." These greatest of all gifts fail of their blessing unless love sets the possessor afire with a passion for helpfulness. "I am nothing," if I possess the gifts without love. We cannot get below or behind nothing.

Verse three of 1 Corinthians 13 speaks of the gift of philanthropy. Paul does not say that philanthropy in itself profits nothing, even though it is unaccompanied with love. A bequest of a million dollars will profit an institution whether bequeathed in anger to rob a hated son, or given in vainglory or ostentation. Philanthropy that blesses a good cause can be used as a selfish instrument to minister to one's hope to be known as a generous soul, or to advertise one's affluence, or to buy one's way into heaven, or to uphold one's image in a business community. But without love, the philanthropy profits the giver nothing. Andrew Fuller once asked an English nobleman for a donation to William Carey's mission endeavor. The nobleman flung in contempt a gold crown on the table in response to the appeal. Andrew Fuller returned it to the rich man, saying: "My Lord demands the heart. Without the heart, I cannot take it." The nobleman felt the rebuke. He accepted the returned gold coin, sat down at his desk and wrote out a generous check for the mission enterprise. "There," he said, "take this; this comes from the heart." James Russell Lowell wrote:

> Not what we give, but what we share,
> For the gift without the giver is bare.

Paul even avows that the gift of the body in a flaming martyrdom can be profitless to the sufferer unless the sacrifice is bestowed in love. Even martyrdom can be but an example of vainglorious (and empty) fanaticism. So many of the early Christian martyrs thus died, seeking for selfish purposes the martyr's crown.

The emphasis Paul makes on the necessity of love in the use of the gifts is presented with dramatic forcefulness. The Apostle holds before our gaze the image of a man whose gifts, graces, and endowments would combine in one person the eloquence of an Apollos (and of a John Chrysostom), the wisdom of a Solomon (and of a Plato), the vision and poetic insight of an Isaiah (and of a Shakespeare), the faith of an Abraham (and of a Martin Luther), the self-sacrifice of a Stephen (and of a Savonarola). Such an incomparably gifted personality! Yet Paul says that if he himself were that man, gathering into his own life all the gifts and graces of these men, it would profit him nothing without the motivation of love. (In his humility Paul arrogates to himself the image of the vain and profitless person. He says not, "You are nothing," but "I am nothing.")

The Characteristics of True Christian Love

The great Apostle now writes in 1 Corinthians 13:4-7 about the characteristics of true Christian love. He defines what this love is. In our English New Testament the word "love" is translated from a number of different Greek words. *Philagathos* is the Greek word for the good (Titus 1:8). *Philadelphia* is the Greek word for love for the brethren (Rom. 12:10; Heb. 13:1). *Philanthropia* is the Greek word for love for mankind (Titus 3:4). *Philotheos* is the Greek word for a lover of God. *Philosophia* is the Greek word for love of wisdom. *Phileo* is love for a friend. *Agape* (John 3:16; 1 John 4:8) is the Greek word for the highest, purest, Godliest love. There is yet another word in the Greek language that was commonly, currently used for love in those ancient times by the philosopher, the poet, the mythologist, and the man on the street. It is the Greek word *eros*. Eros was also the name of the god of love (Latin "Cupid"), the son of Aphrodite (Latin "Venus"). But the word is never found in the Bible. Its use in that ancient world was carnal, sensual, degrading.

The love Paul speaks of here in 1 Corinthians 13 is in a different world from sexual excitement and amorous affection. The word Paul uses is *agape*, the word used to describe God Himself (1 John 4:8). The devoted, consecrated linguist, Jerome, in translating Greek Scriptures into the Latin Vulgate, refused to use the Latin *amor* as an equivalent for the Greek *agape*. The word amor had too many voluptuous overtures. Jerome, therefore, chose the Latin word *caritas* to convey the fulsome meaning. *Caritas* has the connotation of "dearness" in the sense of costliness, esteem, regard, preciousness. Jerome's choice then came into our King James English translation in the word "charity." It refers to the highest love known to God or man, like the love of Jesus for us on the cross (John 3:16).

In 1 Corinthians 13:4-7 Paul describes the holy and heavenly devotion meant by the word *agape* (love). Love, in Paul's definition, is not a weakness but a commitment that bestows strength and character. It is an affection that can sit up all night and say in the morning, "I am not tired." It is the kind of personal joy in service and sacrifice that made the fourteen years Jacob worked for Rachel "seem but a few days, for the love he had to her" (Gen. 29:20). It is the kind of forgiving compassion that causes Ananias in Damascus to come to the persecuting Saul of Tarsus with the loving words, "*Brother Saul . . .*" (Acts 22:12, 13). It is the kind of triumphant spirit that graced the dying testimony of Stephen when he prayed with his last breath for those who took his life, a martyrdom that shook Saul to the depths of his soul (Acts 22:20). This love is the very might and strength of God. It is the *agape*, the *caritas*, the "charity" of 1 Corinthians 13.

133

The Impermanence of Spiritual Gifts

In 1 Corinthians 13:8-13 Paul writes of the impermanence of spiritual gifts and the imperishable nature of love. In verse nine he describes the gifts as being fragments, pieces, portions of a greater whole. In verse ten he says that when the *teleios* is come, when the perfect, the mature, the complete, the full-grown is realized, the fragments of the immature will be no longer necessary. They have become useless. To make an acorn permanent would be to extinguish oak trees forever. To sacrifice an acorn is to get a forest full of them, trees with boughs hanging thick with them. So the gifts are ephemeral, transitional, transitory. They have a use in immaturity, but when maturity is achieved, they are unnecessary.

In verse eleven Paul avows that gifts cease in the sense that they are assimilated into the whole of which they are a part, as the child is done away in the man. The speech of the child (the gift of tongues) is no longer needed in the mature man (the church beyond its infant stage). The understanding of the child (the gift of prophecy) is no longer needed in the full-orbed revelation of God (the church with the completed, written Word). The thinking of the child (the gift of knowledge) is useless in the maturity that accompanies God's final, revealed will (the church with the fullness of inspired revelation). These gifts belong to the infancy, the babyhood of the church. In maturity they are no longer needed.

In verse twelve the Apostle looks forward to the final consummation when all our stumblings and immaturities and incomprehensions are resolved in the perfect clarity of our Lord's full revelation, the Presence of the Saviour Himself. We see now as in an *esoptron*, a polished piece of bronze metal that reflects the image so imperfectly. The ancients had no splendid mirrors of silver-lined glass as we possess today. Their looking glasses were wavy, indistinct, shadowy. Thus they say "as in an *ainigma*," "as in an enigma," "as in an obscure thing." But someday, some glorious day, we shall see and know and understand fully and completely, even as God knows all things.

In verse thirteen Paul triumphantly declares that the three graces of faith, hope, and love shall endure forever, long after all the gifts have ceased and been lost in the fullness of the revelation of God. Faith will be forever the basis for our enjoyment of our Lord. Hope will be forever the forward projection of our expectations and persuasions in God. Love will be forever and unchangeably that in which all things subsist, even faith and hope. Verily, God is love. Love is the greatest of the graces, abiding, imperishable, world without end. With the grace of love in our hearts, every gift of God is a blessing. Giving is a joy, service is a delight, and church is a bit of heaven. We shall not win souls nor mediate the preciousness (caritas) of Christ without love. A professional preacher may not love his parishioners. But without love we can never win souls to Jesus nor worthily exalt our Lord. Isaac Watts has placed in verse the dramatic words of the Apostle Paul.

> Had I the tongues of Greeks and Jews,
> And nobler speech than angels use;
> If love be absent, I am found
> Like tinkling brass, an empty sound.
>
> Were I inspired to preach and tell
> All that is done in heaven and hell;
> Or could my faith the world remove,
> Still I am nothing without love.
>
> Should I distribute all my store
> To feed the hungry, clothe the poor,
> Or give my body to the flame
> To gain a martyr's glorious name.
>
> If love to God and love to man
> Be absent, all my hopes are vain.
> Nor tongues, nor gifts, nor fiery zeal
> The work of love can e'er fulfill.

"And now abideth faith, hope, charity, these three: but the greatest of these is charity."

Chapter 16

The Fruit of the Spirit

Galatians 5

16 This I say then, Walk in the Spirit, and ye shall not fulfill the lust of the flesh.

17 For the flesh lusteth against the Spirit, and the Spirit against the flesh: and these are contrary the one to the other: so that ye cannot do the things that ye would.

18 But if ye be led of the Spirit, ye are not under the law.

19 Now the works of the flesh are manifest, which are these; Adultery, fornication, uncleanness, lasciviousness,

20 Idolatry, witchcraft, hatred, variance, emulations, wrath, strife, seditions, heresies,

21 Envyings, murders, drunkenness, revellings, and such like: of the which I tell you before, as I have also told you in time past, that they which do such things shall not inherit the kingdom of God.

22 But the fruit of the Spirit is love, joy, peace, longsuffering, gentleness, goodness, faith,

23 Meekness, temperance: against such there is no law.

24 And they that are Christ's have crucified the flesh with the affections and lusts.

25 If we live in the Spirit, let us also walk in the Spirit.

26 Let us not be desirous of vain glory, provoking one another, envying one another.

Seven times the Holy Spirit is named in this brief passage of Galatians 5:16-26. Among these instances Paul speaks of walking in the Spirit (5:16), being led by the Spirit (5:18), bearing fruit of the Spirit (5:22), and living in the Spirit (5:25). The text is written against the background of a struggle in our souls. The Apostle writes in 5:17, "For the flesh lusteth [Greek, *epithumeo*, "to desire," "to long for"] against the Spirit and the Spirit against the flesh: and these are contrary the one to the other." The human personality is not of one nature but two. Every man is both good and bad, both light and dark, both of flesh and spirit. This quality of life is greatly heightened in the child of God. Paul describes the torment of the conflict between the old nature of the flesh and the new nature of regeneration in Romans 7:14-24, a passage ending with the agonizing cry, "O wretched man that I am! who shall deliver me from the body of this death?"

The Conflict Between the Old and the New Natures

Paul calls the old nature "the flesh" (Greek, *sarx*). He includes in the word the totality of our depraved, Adamic inheritance. The deep, disturbing depravity of man is tragically portrayed in every page of history and in the daily experience of every human life. We all know the drag of our fleshly passions. The new nature Paul calls the life of the Spirit. When we are born again, we have a new heart, a new love, a new commitment. But the old heart of sin and the old nature of depravity are still with us. Because we are saved does not mean that we are delivered from the passions of the flesh. As long as we live in these mortal bodies, we shall know the trials and temptations that come from the black drops of sin in our blood. Between our two natures there is constant warfare, the flesh against the Spirit and the Spirit against the flesh. Every man is a civil war in his own self. Yea, at the very heart of the universe there is conflict and strife. John writes most vividly in Revelation 12:7, "And there was war in heaven: Michael and his angels fought against the dragon; and the dragon fought and his angels." Nor will this dreadful conflict that involves

137

us all be resolved until Satan is cast into hell at the consummation of the age.

For us to live in these mortal bodies is to know nothing but the agony of sinful conflict. Our worst enemy is ourselves. Augustine frequently prayed, "Lord, deliver me from that evil man, myself." All the fire the devil could bring from Gehenna could do us little harm had we not so much combustible fuel in our hearts. It is the powder in the magazine of our old natures that threatens our spiritual lives with daily disaster. Our perpetual foe is ourselves. Our worst sins are those that arise out of the depravity of our souls. Cain killed his brother Abel because God made a difference between the sacrifices of the two. The brothers of Joseph hated him because they had no coat of many colors. Saul the king sulked in his tent, eaten up of jealousy, as he heard the women of Israel sing, "Saul hath slain his thousands but David his tens of thousands." Judas, coveting for his mercenary life all he could retrieve out of a lost cause, sold his Lord for thirty pieces of silver. The elder brother, in the parable told by Jesus, refused to come into the house because the younger, prodigal son had been welcomed back home. It is a sorry picture, this picture of depraved human nature, this life of the flesh.

Look at Galatians 5:22. "But," Paul says in effect, "there is something more, there is something besides, there is something better." How meaningful that little word "but" can sometimes be, that distinctive conjunction, that dividing monosyllable! "But the fruit of the Spirit is love, joy, peace. . . ." Our evil natures may be capable of the worst and the darkest of sins, but the Holy Spirit of God within us is the power of heaven to make us fruitful unto righteousness. We who are saved can know also the glorious fruit of the Spirit.

Notice that in Galatians 5:19 Paul uses a plural word to describe the life of the flesh. "Now the works [plural] of the flesh are manifest." But in Galatians 5:

138

22 the Apostle uses the singular to describe the life of the Spirit. "But the fruit [singular] of the Spirit. . . ." The works of the flesh are many, dark and devious. Paul names seventeen of them in this list recorded in Galatians 5:19-21, and after he has named the monstrous brood, he adds the words "and such like," as if to say he could have added five hundred more even more repulsive. The works of the flesh are a ferment of confused, contradictory, conflicting depredations. Each one but contends against another for an evil mastery. It is not so with the fruit of the Spirit. The fruit of the Spirit is one, singular. All throughout is consistent. One grace does not take away from another grace, but rather each one contributes to the richness and beauty of the whole. Whether known by the name of love or joy or meekness, yet all are one because of the Holy Spirit in our hearts.

The life that produces these marvelous graces is not of us but of God. They are not the product (Moffatt calls them the "harvest") of natural generation but of supernatural regeneration. In our natural, human strength we sometimes try to exhibit these graces. We obey laws, make resolutions, observe rules, enter periods of reformation, seek to make ourselves over. All these attempts at goodness only emphasize our ultimate failure. We are like the prisoner pardoned out of the penitentiary but back again after three months for the same offense. We in ourselves cannot change ourselves. If the tree is evil, the fruit is evil. But what we cannot do in ourselves, the Holy Spirit does for us. He is in the sanctifying business and He is the One who can remake our lives, giving us strength for weakness, victory for defeat, and enriching us with the nine graces of holy blessedness. But the life that exhibits this fruit must be rooted in the Spirit, quickened by the Spirit, alive in the Spirit. There is never fruit out of a dead tree. Dead posts produce no fruit. These beautiful graces cannot be outwardly hung upon a life like toys and ornaments upon a Christmas tree. Fruitage in the Spirit requires rootage in the Spirit.

The normal life of the child of God ensues in this heavenly fruit. We are not surprised to find apples on an apple tree or grapes hanging down from a grapevine. We would be surprised and disappointed if there were no apples on the apple tree and no grapes hanging down from the vine. In the parable told by our Lord in Luke 13:6-9, the husbandman who found no figs on his fig tree for three years demanded that it be cut down, "for why cumbereth it the ground?" In Matthew 21:18-20 Jesus cursed the fig tree that bare nothing but leaves. In John 15:8 our Lord said, "Herein is my Father glorified, that ye bear much fruit: so shall ye be my disciples." If we have been born again and if we love God, we shall exhibit those nine graces, the loving fruit of the Spirit.

The Nine Gifts of the Spirit and the Nine Graces of the Spirit

There are nine gifts of the Spirit listed in 1 Corinthians 12:8-10. There are nine graces of the Spirit listed in Galatians 5:22, 23. What are the differences between the gifts of the Spirit and the graces of the Spirit? The differences are most apparent. The ninefold gifts of the Spirit are for power, service and ministry. The ninefold graces are for Christian character, for what the child of God is in himself. The nine gifts are distributed among the members of the congregation, one here, two there, three yonder. The nine graces are to be represented in every Christian. They are but facets of the same glorious gem. The nine gifts are sovereignly bestowed. We may ask for a gift, but the Holy Spirit chooses as to whether our request is accepted or denied. The nine graces crown all who walk in the Spirit. The Spirit does not choose among them. They all are ours — fully, richly, everlastingly.

A gift may enjoy perfect expression even though it

140

is a solitary one bestowed upon the individual. But no grace can enjoy perfect expression if it is not accompanied by every other member in the list. Love, for example, is not complete if it is not accompanied by the grace of long-suffering. ("Love suffereth long," 1 Cor. 13:4). Love is not complete if it is not accompanied by the grace of gentleness, kindness ("Love is kind," 1 Cor. 13:4). Love is not complete if it is not accompanied by the grace of meekness ("Love vaunteth not itself, is not puffed up," 1 Cor. 13:4). Love is not complete if it is not accompanied by the grace of temperance ("Love doth not behave itself unseemly," 1 Cor. 13:5). Love is not complete if it is not accompanied by the grace of peace ("Love is not easily provoked," 1 Cor. 13:5). Love is not complete if it is not accompanied by the grace of goodness ("Love thinketh no evil," 1 Cor. 13:5). Love is not complete if it is not accompanied by the grace of joy ("Love rejoiceth not in iniquity, but rejoiceth in the truth," 1 Cor. 13:6). Love is not complete if it is not accompanied by the grace of faith ("Love believeth all things," 1 Cor. 13:7). The nine graces are inseparable. To possess one, we must surely possess all. They are the fruit (singular) of the Spirit.

When we look at these nine graces closely. we notice that they easily fall into three groups of three. The first triad pertains to our relation to God: love, joy, peace. The second triad depicts our relation to others: longsuffering, gentleness, goodness. The third triad presents our relation to ourselves: faith, meekness, temperance. These three trilogies are both Godward and manward. They are both perpendicular and horizontal. They come down from God and flow toward man.

The Fruit of the Spirit
Described in the Nine Graces

The first of the nine graces is love (Greek, *agape*). Love heads the list, as we know after reading 1 Corinthians 13:1-13. This is in perfect keeping with the teaching of our Lord in Matthew 22:35-40: "Then one of them, which was a lawyer, asked him a question, tempting him, and saying, Master, which is the great commandment in the law? Jesus said unto him, Thou shalt love the Lord thy God with all thy heart, and with all thy soul, and with all thy mind. This is the first and great commandment. And the second is like unto it, Thou shalt love thy neighbour as thyself. On these two commandments hang all the law and the prophets." Paul later added, "Love worketh no ill to his neighbour: therefore love is the fulfilling of the law" (Rom. 13:10). Our Saviour said to His disciples, "By this shall all men know that ye are my disciples, if ye have love one to another" (John 13:35). Love is of God for verily "God is love" (1 John 4:8). Love makes us want to do what once we felt we had to do.

The second grace is joy (Greek, *chara*). In the light of the New Testament this is an amazing virtue. Look at Paul's letter to the Thessalonians in 1 Thessalonians 1:6, where he speaks of that faithful congregation as "having received the word in much affliction, with joy of the Holy Ghost." Do those two words go together? *Affliction* and *joy?* The world would not think so. Late on a Thursday night, before He was to be crucified at 9:00 the next morning, Jesus spoke to His disciples about His "joy" (John 15:11; 16:22). What "joy" could there be in the agony of crucifixion? Hebrews 12:2 describes that amazing and heavenly phenomenon, "joy" in the presence of shame and suffering and death. When Paul and Silas were beaten until their backs were crimsoned in blood, when they were placed in stocks and in chains and thrown into the innermost part of a dungeon, at midnight they prayed and sang praises to God. What kind of "joy" was that? No wonder "the prisoners heard them" (Acts 16:25). The pastor of the church at Jerusalem, James, the Lord's brother, wrote in his epistle, "My brethren, count it all joy when ye fall into divers temptations [trials]" (James 1:2). It is the first thing that he said in his letter. What kind of a "joy" is this? Only the Christian knows. The world has merriment, laughter, entertainment, revelry, but only the Christian knows "joy." Bars and stone walls and fagots and persecution cannot take it from him. It is the joy of the presence of God in the soul.

The third grace is peace (Greek, *eirene*). Thus Paul writes in Romans 5:1, "Therefore being justified by faith, we have peace with God through our Lord Jesus Christ." This is "the peace of God which passeth all understanding," which keeps our hearts and minds through Christ Jesus (Phil. 4:7).

The fourth grace is long-suffering (Greek, *makro-thumia*). In the presence of wrong and persecution, we are to be patient and full of forbearance. We are to wait on God for *His* justification (Rom. 12:19). In a world of speed, we are to be slow to take offense and we are to leave vengeance in the hands of the Lord.

The fifth grace is gentleness (Greek, *chrestotes*). It is the kindness so beautifully spoken of in Ephesians 4:32, "Be ye kind one to another, tenderhearted, forgiving one another even as God for Christ's sake hath forgiven you."

The sixth grace is goodness (Greek, *agathosune*). Thus Barnabas is described in Acts 11:24, "For he was a good man, and full of the Holy Ghost and of faith." That would be a worthy epitaph upon the tombstone of any man.

The seventh grace is faith (Greek, *pistis*). This is the only one found in both the lists of gifts in 1 Corinthians 12:9 and the list of graces in Galatians 5:22. Faith, the gift, is for power, for doing great things in the name of the Lord (Mark 11:23; James 5:16-18). Faith, the grace, is for character, the gift of resting in God, free from cankering care and corroding anxiety.

We exercise the gift of faith when we accept the promises of God and attempt to do great things for Him. We exhibit the grace of faith when we quiet our hearts before the Lord and trust in Him who is able to keep us forever.

The eighth grace is meekness (Greek, *praiotes*). In our bearing toward others, we are to exhibit mildness, gentleness. Thus Moses is described as being the meekest man in all the world (Num. 12:3). Thus Jesus said the meek shall inherit the earth (Matt. 5:5).

The last and the ninth grace is temperance (Greek, *egkrateia*). The word means self-control. It is the victory of the Spirit over the flesh.

Someone has said these graces are a portrait of Christ. That is so true. But Paul was painting a portrait of us who name the name of Jesus. May God grant that the beauty of this life of the Spirit may shine forth in all of our ways to the glory of our blessed Saviour. Amen.